ACCIDENTS IN NORTH AMERICAN MOUNTAINEERING

VOLUME 7 • NUMBER 1 • ISSUE 49

1996

THE AMERICAN ALPINE CLUB
GOLDEN

THE ALPINE CLUB OF CANADA
BANFF

ISSN 0065-082X

ISBN 0-930-410-63-7

Manufactured in the United States of America

Published by
The American Alpine Club, Inc.
710 Tenth Street
Golden, CO 80401

Cover Illustration
A sunny weekend morning on the Lower Slabs of White Horse Ledges outside Conway, New Hampshire. A popular destination (count 'em), where some people wear helmets— for good reason. Photograph by Peter Lewis.

♻ Printed on recycled paper

CONTENTS

SAFETY COMMITTEES 1995

The American Alpine Club

Dr. Benjamin G. Ferris, Jr. (Honorary), John Dill, George Hurley, Jeff Sheetz, Fred Stanley, James Yester, and John E. (Jed) Williamson *(Chairman)*

The Alpine Club of Canada

Helmut Microys, Orvel Miskiw, Frank Pianka, Paul Ritzema, Michael Swanguard, Harvey Struss, and Murray Toft *(Chairman)*

ACCIDENTS IN
NORTH AMERICAN MOUNTAINEERING

Forty-Ninth Annual Report of the
Safety Committees of The American Alpine Club
and The Alpine Club of Canada

This is the forty-ninth issue of *Accidents in North American Mountaineering*, published by the AAC, and the eighteenth that has been done with The Alpine Club of Canada.

Canada: The wet summer of 1995 suppressed climbing activity, especially mountaineering, in much of Canada. Correspondingly, the statistics show a light and even distribution of accidents through most of the year, with a norm of one per month, rising slightly in July and August as the usual summer vacation peaks. However, particularly fine weather arrived in September, and predictably, pent-up throngs of deprived climbers rushed out to make up for lost time. The result was a flurry of accidents in September. Again, the predominant causes were falls with inadequate safety systems, and rappel failures and errors.

We continually strive to improve coverage of the country for accounts of climbing accidents, and welcome a number of new reporters. We also thank the several people who have taken the time to write and send us their personal stories of involvement in accidents, often painful to do. Including the above with our regular reporters, we thank the following people for their help this year: Tim Auger, Steve Blake, Yves Bosse, Martin Brenner, Eric Dafoe, George Field, Harry Fischer, Lloyd Freese, Clair Israelson, Marc Ledwidge, Garth Lemke, Brian Merry, Amie Nashalik, Jean-Claude Néolet, Richard Parson, Shawn Shea, and Robert Stock. Our regrets to anyone we've missed.

United States: Everything goes in cycles, which in the case of causes for climbing accidents is unfortunate. Nothing could be more illustrative of this than the category "Rappel Failure/Error." The number of reports in this category had been in a fairly steady decline, with some spikes, the average having been five per year for the past decade. The two most common errors in the earlier years were rappelling off the end of one's rope and having the rappel anchor "fail." These were corrected by tying a knot in the end of the rappel rope and having more than one anchor point if the primary protection is not deemed to be bomb proof.

Last year there were twelve reports and this year there are fifteen that are attributed to rappel problems. They are mostly of a different nature than in the past, and at least half of them occurred on top-rope climbs. The major causes include: having doubled ropes uneven causing rappeller to experience entire rope slipping through the top anchor; rappel rope not being long enough to reach the bottom; climber not anchoring while setting up the rappel; not belaying beginning climbers or using a prussik as a back up; and misusing the rappel device—such as incorrect threading of rappel rope, and having the ropes jam so that they are irretrievable—thus stranding the climbers. The few cases involving hair or clothes caught in belay devices and neophytes not being belayed can only be attributed to ignoring basic principles. Coupled with all of these are some contributory factors that need to be recognized. First is the problem of distraction. Many of the accidents occurred in areas with many other climbers nearby, so attention to the details at hand were in competition with conversation. Second seems to be the problem of haste. Climbers have either started late in the day and want to get off before dark, or they are just plain in a hurry to get down and on to the next event (such as a meeting with friends in the bar, as one fellow admitted). Upon closer scrutiny, there seems to be a more subtle third cause: proximity to the roadhead. That is, the vast majority of these accidents took place in climbing areas that are just off the road. Many of the climbers involved have indicated that even though they were aware of the technical aspects of rappelling, they did not pay as close attention as they might have if they were hours or days from civilization.

California certainly had its share of weather related problems again this year. In Steve Roper's book, *Camp Four*, there is the story about Galen Rowell pulling out a sleeping bag at a bivouac site back in the 60's and being instantly chastised by T. M. Herbert for being such a wimp. None of the Yosemite climbers of that time would be caught with much more than a wool sweater and hat in their packs. Now there are portaledges and synthetics that breathe and allegedly don't leak. So why are there so many weather related rescues on El Capitan these days? Part of it has to do with a general level of unpreparedness, and for that reason, the Park is citing climbers more often for "creating a hazardous condition." It would be appropriate for other parks and the USFS to consider using this approach a bit more often.

In addition to the Safety Committee, we are grateful to the following individuals for collecting data and helping with the report: Hank Alicandri, Elliot Crooks, Micki Canfield, Jim Detterline, Gary Guenther, Charlie Logan, John Markwell, Tom McCrumm, Daniel Miskinis, Daryl Miller, Rich Perch, Roger Robinson, Steven Schmelzer, Jim Underwood, and, of course, George Sainsbury.

John E. (Jed) Williamson
Editor, USA
7 River Ridge
Hanover, NH 03755
USA

Orvel Miskiw
Editor, Canada
5 Meskanaw Road
R.R. 2 Cochrane
Alberta TOL OWO
CANADA

CANADA

INADEQUATE PROTECTION—ICE TOOL CAME OUT, FATIGUE, EXCEEDING ABILITIES
Alberta, Rocky Mountains, Ghost River, "This House of Sky" Falls

About 1600 on January 28, after several satisfactory hours of ice climbing, G. R. and R. P. were attempting a pitch near the top of "This House of Sky." They intended to complete that pitch, rappel down, and then descend a walk-out route to complete their day. After climbing the first five meters, G. R. found a solid stance and ax placement, and set up to place the first ice screw with his right hand. While he was doing that, the ice around his left tool fractured in a large dinner plate, and the tool pulled. G. R. fell to the bottom of the pitch, and slid down the snow slope until the rope stopped him. He suffered a simple fracture of both bones of the lower left leg just above the ankle. Another party was on the route. They assisted in stabilizing G. R. and went out of their way to ensure that he was comfortable, and to help R. P. with arranging helicopter evacuation for G. R., through Kananaskis Emergency Services. Because of the remoteness of the location, the rescue was not completed until well past optimum light for flying. G. R. reached Canmore Hospital at about 1720.

Analysis

These intermediate climbers had been climbing together for two years, but this was only their second outing of the season, and both were using unfamiliar ice tools, in which a lack of confidence had developed during the day. Also, both were somewhat fatigued when they reached the last pitch, and knew it would stretch their technical skills. Unfortunately, none of these concerns were mentioned at the time. The desire to complete the climb on a high note took precedence. A party should discuss its plans and limitations before setting out. (Source: Climber R. P.)

AVALANCHE, EXCEEDING ABILITIES, WEATHER
Alberta, Rocky Mountains, Cascade Mountain, "Urs Hole" Falls

Sometime on February 24, two ice climbers (both 20) were hit by an avalanche while climbing the waterfall route "Urs Hole", near Banff. Both died. One body was located the next day; the other was not recovered until the following summer.

The Urs Hole is a deep gully containing several ice steps leading up to a 25-meter, grade-three pitch. This gully is below a huge bowl that drains much of the South Face of Cascade Mountain. Unseasonably mild and stormy conditions were predicted for the day of the climb, and in fact a drizzle set in around noon and continued until the next morning. The climbers had started out around mid-morning, so they likely reached the key pitch, well up the gully, after the rainfall had begun.

Friends and wardens approached the foot of the gully on the evening the two were reported overdue, but the route was too dangerous for a search. The body of G. L. was spotted from the air early the next morning, but recovering it was difficult because the avalanche danger was still extreme. G. L. was hanging by his seat harness from an anchor below a block. His tools, pack, hat, and a mitt were all gone, but he seemed to be relatively uninjured. His death was likely caused at least partly by hypothermia. The doubled rope was hanging near him from a rock bolt about 25 meters higher up, at the top of the main pitch, but there was no sign of S. M.

The avalanche deposit in the narrow canyon immediately below was estimated to be more than 15 meters deep. A brief search was conducted that day, using the Parks Canada dog team, and the gully was searched three days later during a cold snap, by which time the snow had frozen solid, making digging impossible.

A few personal articles were later found in search attempts through the spring, and the helicopter was used to check the gully during the summer. Eventually, S. M.'s body was found, about 50 meters below the main pitch, when the snow melted away from it in a moat along a rock face. He had been at least ten meters below the surface. S. M. had apparently been swept off the falls by a large fresh slide. It is possible he had been rappelling at the time and was carried off the end of the ropes.

Analysis
The guidebook description of this route begins, "Don't even look at this route after the first significant snowfalls of the year." The day these climbers selected was likely the worst one of the season, with the snowpack affected by warm weather and rain.

S. M. had started ice climbing the previous winter when he had first come to Banff, and had climbed other routes on Cascade a number of times previously, but this was G. L.'s first ice climb, and equipment had been borrowed for him to go along.

Both climbers were local staff. Safety information given by the Parks Service is prepared with a view to reducing incidents like this. (Source: Tim Auger, Banff National Park Warden Service)

FALL ON ICE, INADEQUATE BELAY POSITION, PROTECTION PULLED OUT
Alberta, Rocky Mountains, Lake Louise, Louise Falls
A party of two were climbing the upper pillar (grade V) of this popular waterfall on March 20, About ten meters out from the belay, the leader fell, pulling out the one screw he had placed for protection. The resulting 20-meter fall was arrested by his belayer, but the force of the fall spun him around and he sustained a fractured fibula. The leader was not injured. The two climbers were assisted to the base of the waterfall by an ACMG Guide who was working in the area, and then the injured climber was slung out by helicopter to an ambulance waiting at Lake Louise. (Source: Marc Ledwidge, Banff National Park Warden Service)

Analysis
Belays should be set up so they transfer impacts from all likely directions to the anchor in as straight a line as possible. The belayer then needs only to control the run of the rope. (Source: Orvel Miskiw)

FALL ON ROCK, INADEQUATE PROTECTION
Alberta, Rocky Mountains, Cougar Canyon
About 1500 on May 13, Kananaskis E.M.S. received a call regarding an injured rock climber up Cougar Creek. They notified Park rangers and Canmore Fire Department, then left for the scene. The ranger on duty directed a colleague to Cougar Canyon im-

mediately while he gathered appropriate rescue equipment and called Alpine Helicopters to stand by.

When the first ranger reached the accident site, he found that climber M. S. had fallen off a 5.11 route on Catseye Cliff Left above the second bolt, and dropped about three meters onto a tree top. His inner thigh had been impaled by the old broken top of the tree. He sustained a three-centimeter flesh wound. He was evacuated to the trailhead, where his friends drove him to Canmore Hospital. (Source: George Field, Kananaskis Country Alpine Specialist)

OVERDUE, WEATHER POOR NAVIGATION, CLIMBING ALONE
Alberta, Rocky Mountains, Columbia Ice Field

On July 22, D. E.(52) started up the Athabasca Glacier on his way to Mt. Columbia, and reached its summit (3748 meters) in a whiteout at 1600. Starting out toward the road, he bivvied on the ice field south of Snow dome. Next morning he broke camp at 1000, intending to descend the Athabasca Glacier, but again in a whiteout, he got disoriented and reached steep terrain south of Mt. Andromeda. Then, thinking he was somewhere to the north, he turned south, hoping to descend Saskatchewan Glacier; however, in reality he was heading down Castle Guard Glacier. Continuing well below tree line, he realized something was wrong, turned back, and camped that night below the glacier. On July 24, he started traveling at 0500, got his bearings sorted out, and was on his way to Athabasca Glacier at 1250 when he was located and picked up, in good condition, by Jasper Park wardens. (Source: Steve Blake, Jasper National Park Warden Service)

Analysis

D. E. had intermediate experience and good equipment, but apart from the simplicity of independent travel, soloing in the Columbia Icefields has little to recommend it, and is discouraged because of the hazards involved. In this case, D. E. managed to avoid them. (Source: Orvel Miskiw)

FALL ON ROCK, INADEQUATE PROTECTION, HANDHOLD FAILURE
Alberta, Rocky Mountains, Kid Goat Buttress, "Keelhaul Wall"

On July 24, Laura and Marty went to the Canadian Rockies for a climbing trip, hoping to do a few routes in the Bow Corridor. Starting at Kid Goat Buttress, they had a good time on "Twilight Zone," found the north descent gully, and then proceeded up "Keelhaul Wall," another 5.6.

They combined the first two pitches into one with their 60-meter rope, and then on the third pitch, Marty continued past the trees, as it seemed better to belay a little higher up. Unfortunately it was hard to find a good belay stance, and when he did, his three placements were spread far apart and so he had to use the rope to link them all together. That made it difficult to rearrange for Laura to take over the belay, so she decided to lead the last pitch. That pitch was rated 5.5, and Laura was solid on 5.7's, so they were confident she could do it.

Leading out, Laura found a slot about five meters up, but all she could get into it was a #1 Rock, which she did not think was any good. She climbed on, over the crux, unable to find or place any more protection, and about nine meters above her only protection, she was feeling secure again when an apparently solid hold broke off in her hand. She fell 15 meters down the rock until the rope came tight through her only protection placement. Screaming in pain when she stopped, Laura managed to climb some five meters back up to the belay.

Her apparent injuries included sprains of both ankles, a sprained thumb, cuts and abrasions of both hands, and abrasions of her seat. Marty put a jacket on her and gave her water, then lowered her down the route, leaving behind a few pitons, several slings, and a lot of blood. He was amazed at how well she endured the descent, as she could not use her hands, but had to use her injured ankles throughout. At the base, Marty taped up Laura's worst ankle, took all their heavy gear in his pack, and helped her to walk out to the road before dark, at about 2200. He then drove her to Canmore Hospital, where she was checked over, given first aid, and told to come back in the morning for X-rays. She had no fractures, but two badly strained finger tendons added to the list of her injuries. (Source: Marty)

Analysis
Laura was wearing a helmet and day pack, which protected her head and back when she fell. The sparse protection may have made her impatient after the crux moves, and may have caused her to rely on handholds without testing them. (Source: Orvel Miskiw)

FALL ON ICE, PLACED NO PROTECTION
Alberta, Rocky Mountains, Mount Aberdeen
About 1700 on August 27, a party of four were descending the north glacier separating the summits of Mts. Aberdeen (3152 meters) and Haddo. On the lower ice tongue (angled about 38 degrees), they were tied in on separate ropes, with R. T. and A. B. descending together on one of them, separated about 20 meters. R. T., who was higher, fell and pulled A. B. off. They both slid about 60 meters onto lower-angled ice, where A. B. managed to self-arrest short of the rocks beyond the glacier. R. T. suffered leg and ankle fractures as well as serious chest injuries likely caused by an ice ax, while A. B. sustained minor knee injuries. They were helped down by their two companions, and a member of another party nearby went out for help and reported the accident to the Banff Warden Service about 1900. The climbers were evacuated by heli-sling and transferred to Banff EMS before nightfall. R. T. was diagnosed with serious internal bleeding, and would likely not have survived the night if he had not been hospitalized.

Analysis
When traveling on bare ice, even with crampons, it is very difficult to self-arrest, or to hold any type of fall without a belay, even on moderate terrain such as this glacier on Mt. Aberdeen. If a rope is necessary for safety, then the use of belays and/or protection is usually required as well. (Source: Marc Ledwidge, Banff National Park Warden Service)

FALL ON ROCK, UNROPED
Alberta, Rocky Mountains, Mount Indefatigable
On September 5, Kananaskis Country rangers were informed that someone had fallen down the East Face of Mt. Indefatigable (2670 meters) from the ridge joining its two peaks. A helicopter was requested, and a search and rescue operation proceeded in bad weather conditions, involving several rangers and Kananaskis Emergency Medical Services. At 1519, about one hour after the initial report was received, J. A., a visitor from

Scotland, was found at 2317 meters on the east face of the mountain, having fallen some 300 meters to her death. Park rangers were transported to her position by helicopter sling to investigate and remove the body to Kananaskis EMS. (Source: George Field, Kananaskis Country Alpine Specialist)

Analysis

J. A. had many years of scrambling experience in Scotland and Europe, and it's not known why she fell. Although her companion reported that conditions were a "reasonable Scottish mist," he says the rock was not slippery. The traverse of Mt. Indefatigable is considered a moderate scramble, and such a rating may lead some to think it presents little or no hazard. But the serious exposure in one or two spots is ample reason to take along a rope and use it to belay in those places. (Source: Orvel Miskiw)

RAPPEL FAILURE—ERROR IN ANCHORING, INEXPERIENCE
Alberta, Rocky Mountains, Mount Rundle

On September 10, David and Edward, (both 18), from England, and temporary employees of the Banff Springs Hotel, were rock climbing on the lower ridge of Mt. Rundle when an accident occurred in which David fell to his death.

They had climbed easy fifth-class rock about 175 meters above the local practice area, and then moved around onto the east face to rappel off the ridge to easy ground. Edward, the less experienced of the two, states they located a rappel anchor which consisted of a large horn or boulder with a sling around it. David, however, decided to remove and keep the sling, and instead looped the rope directly over the rock. Both climbers then rappelled moderate-angled slabs to a ledge lower on the face.

When they tried to retrieve the rope, it jammed. David decided to climb back up to free the rope. Edward believes David tied himself in to the rope as a safety measure, as he climbed up easily and out of Edward's sight near the top of the pitch. A few minutes later, Edward heard a noise, and saw David fall past him and land on ledges below. The full rope fell with him. Edward called for help and the Park Service and ambulance personnel were summoned.

Analysis

David was out of sight of his partner at the time he fell, so the exact cause is unknown. Edward says he understood that David was going to free the rope and toss it down the pitch rather than rappel. However, when his body was recovered, the rope was rigged as if for rappel or self-belay through a Sticht plate attached to his harness, so it's quite possible that David was setting up to rappel again when he fell. In any case, while both climbers had rappelled before, they were new to this area and may not have been familiar with jammed ropes, a common problem in the Rockies because of the nature of the rock. (Source: Tim Auger, Banff National Park Warden Service)

FALL ON ROCK, UNROPED, NO HARD HAT
Alberta, Rocky Mountains, Tonquin Valley, Surprise Point

Two Japanese members of an Indian Summer Alpine Club Camp at the Wates-Gibson Hut climbed and scrambled up fourth-class terrain of the northeast aspect of Surprise Point (2400 meters) to a peak on its north ridge on September 13. After surmounting some short cliffs, they reached the top at about 1300.

As they were starting to descend, basically along their ascent route, they separated slightly to check for the best way to go. While doing that, J. N. (76) apparently slipped. He fell some 120 meters down the cliffs onto a scree slope, hitting his head and sustaining numerous severe fractures on the way. He was likely killed instantly. His partner, H. K., worked his way down to him, determined that J. N. was fatally injured, and then went to the hut for help. A member of the camp ran out to the road and reported the accident about five hours later.

A rescue team of two flew in to the hut, where the surviving partner and another camp member gave them a good description of the location of the victim, having just returned from wrapping up the body and marking its location. The rescuers were slung to the site by helicopter, and recovered the body as daylight was fading.

Analysis
An older man, J. N. had done quite a number of easy climbs, and attended Alpine Club camps for the past seven years. As well, Alpine Club members had visited Japan to climb with him. It's not known what information he and H. K. had obtained, about their intended route, but they carried no rope or helmets on this outing, although it was definitely more challenging than just a walk-up. A third person who had started up with them turned back earlier, as he felt that the route was "too dangerous". A rope and a good knowledge of short-roping could have been put to good use here, and wearing a helmet may have prevented fatal injuries. (Source: Steve Blake, Jasper National Park Warden Service)

SLIP ON SNOW, NO HARD HAT
Alberta, Rocky Mountains, Mount Haddo
After a successful ascent of Mt. Haddo (3071 meters) on September 16, a party of three were descending a gully system toward Paradise Valley from the Haddo-Aberdeen saddle, when the highest climber lost his footing on the snow and slid onto the others, knocking them down. They all stopped eventually, but the climber who fell first suffered an injury to his head when he struck it on a rock. The climbers had removed their helmets for the descent. One companion hiked out and alerted Parks Canada officials, and the victim and the third party member were evacuated by helicopter later that day.

Analysis
As snow softens later in the day, the potential for slipping and then rapidly accelerating increases. In this instance, keeping the helmets on for the descent may have lessened the injuries. (Source: Marc Ledwidge, Banff National Park Warden Service)

OVERDUE, DIFFICULTY FOLLOWING ROUTE,
POOR CONDITIONS—SNOW, INEXPERIENCE, FROSTBITE
Alberta, Rocky Mountains, Mount Edith Cavell
On September 30, G. M. (30) and partner (39) climbed the East Ridge of Mt. Edith Cavell (3363 meters). The route was in poor condition, with snow. Although adequately equipped, they were relatively inexperienced and had trouble with route finding. A 40-hour round trip resulted.

Meanwhile, the climbers were reported overdue, and a helicopter search was undertaken the following day. They were located returning on the trail, about five kilometers from the road. They had both sustained some frostbite, one to his hands, and the other to his toes. (Source: Steve Blake, Jasper National Park Warden Service)

Analysis
Cavell's East Ridge is considered a one-day climb, though it's usually a full day. Late returns are usual and bivouacs common. Good research on it is more important than for many other mountain climbs, and inexperienced climbers especially are advised to get a detailed description of the entire circuit from someone familiar with the route, then take a reconnaissance hike to the base, and start well before ˙ dawn on the day of their climb. Though a moderate challenge overall, it contains a number of potential snags which can cause unnecessary delays. (Source: Orvel Miskiw)

RAPPEL FAILURE—INADEQUATE ANCHOR SETUP, INADEQUATE EQUIPMENT
Alberta, Lake Louise, Back of the Lake Crag
On October 6, a climber was being lowered by her partner in order to retrieve her protection slings after leading the route "Top Gun" (5.7). After descending about 15 meters, she reached the lower-angled section of the climb and removed the last runner. A short distance below that, she fell five meters to the ground, suffering a deep puncture wound to the lower back, and a fractured tailbone. She was treated for her injuries and flown out by helicopter, by the Banff Warden Service and paramedics.

Analysis
The master point at the anchor was a steel, marine-type non-locking carabiner. The victim had clipped her rope in to it for lowering. Upon reaching the easier-angled rock, she may have partly unweighted the rope. It appears that the rope or the anchor carabiner changed position, and the rope ran across the gate of the carabiner and unclipped from it. A carabiner has the advantage that the climber does not have to untie to pass the rope through it, but as in various other situations, a single non-locking carabiner should be considered inadequate as the only point of attachment, as the potential exists for the rope to unclip itself. (Source: Marc Ledwidge, Banff National Park Warden Service)

FALLING ICE, POOR POSITION
Alberta, Rocky Mountains, Weeping Wall
On December 29, two ice climbers were on the second pitch of the left side of the Weeping Wall (grade IV) when the leader dislodged a chunk of ice onto his belayer. The victim, a 19-year old university student, was wearing a helmet, but was struck on the back of the head when he ducked, and was knocked unconscious. It was a busy day at the Weeping Wall, and nearby climbers helped to lower him to the base of the climb. He was evacuated to Banff by helicopter, and then transferred to hospital in Calgary. He had suffered a severe concussion, but recovered.

Analysis
Proper location of the belay is one of the essential skills in waterfall climbing, since falling ice is almost a certainty. The main variable is the amount. On an open face like this, the belay should be off to one side, the longer the pitch, the more to the side. If the

belayer still finds himself in the line of fire, he can obtain additional protection by holding a pack over his head, especially jamming it against the ice wall to eliminate an opening where debris could bounce off and hit him.

The Weeping Wall is one of the most popular ice climbing areas in the Canadian Rockies, with an approach of just a few minutes from the road on a packed trail. But it is about 160 kilometers from the nearest hospital, and emergency response time is at least 1.5 hours. Add to this the travel time of the reporting person to the nearest telephone, and the serious implications of a head injury become obvious. (Source: Tim Auger, Banff National Park Warden Service)

FALL INTO BERGSCHRUND, UNROPED, POOR VISIBILITY
British Columbia, Bugaboo Glacier, Howser Spires
On September 3, R. D. and K. S. completed a new route on North Howser Spire (3400 meters), and after most of the descent, were unroped on a low-angled snow and rock slope about 200 meters from the relatively flat glacier. K. S. decided to glissade the rest of the way, even though the surrounding terrain showed bergschrunds at the bases of most rock slopes.

After sliding about 45 meters, he went over the upper wall of a 'schrund, and fell some six meters onto a small bench, where he landed on his back. R. D. saw him disappear from view, then traversed around to reach him by an easier route, and found K. S. conscious and lucid, but slightly shocky and unable to move his legs. They decided that R. D. would go out and report the accident. Walking through a badly crevassed area to reach the Bugaboo-Snowpatch Col, he relayed a message to climbers at the bottom. K. S. was helicoptered out the following morning.

Analysis
These two climbers had adequate equipment and experience, but the flat light deceived K. S. into thinking the slope was continuous. He was fortunate that the night weather was warm and stable, and that his partner was able to reach help across a dangerously crevassed glacier. Had R. D. fallen into a hole, he would not have been reported missing until two days later, by friends, as the climbers had not informed Park rangers of their plans. Possibly through elation at their success, J. S.'s judgment did not allow for the hazards they still faced on their return, especially in view of the minimal party size. (Source: Garth Lemke, Bugaboo Provincial Park; and Orvel Miskiw)

FALL ON ROCK, UNROPED, HANDHOLD CAME OFF
British Columbia, Rocky Mountains, Mount Assiniboine
On September 21, two climbers were beginning the standard North Ridge route of Mt. Assiniboine (3620 meters). The route was in excellent late-season condition with hard firm snow, which necessitated the use of crampons for the entire ascent, including short mixed sections. After stepping off the initial snow slopes, they started climbing a short step of loose fourth-class rock. About three meters up, the lower climber pulled off a loose handhold and fell backward onto the 35-degree snow slope, then slid down about 100 meters, catching a crampon on the way.

The crampon came off her boot. Her partner helped her to get back to the Hind Hut at the base of the route and then descended to Lake Magog to request help. The victim was evacuated later in the day, by helicopter. She sustained a third-degree knee sprain and a first-degree ankle sprain.

Analysis
Both climbers were very experienced and comfortable soloing on this terrain, but loose rock is typical for the range, and in this case the use of a rope may have prevented the injury. She was unable to self arrest because her ice ax had been put away before they started up the rock. (Source: Marc Ledwidge, Banff National Park Warden Service)

FALL ON RAPPEL—NO BELAY, INEXPERIENCE
Nova Scotia, Eagle's Nest
On April 13, Chris and Ray went out to this popular climbing area to do some basic top-roping. They decided to rappel to the bottom of the 20-meter cliff, even though Chris was not very experienced at rappelling. Chris went first, and after descending about ten meters, her right foot slipped, sending her swinging against the wall with her right side. Surprised, she made the mistake of releasing the rope with her brake hand in order to steady herself, and she immediately began to fall. In a desperate attempt to stop herself, she grabbed the rope in her hands. Although she fell all the way to the bottom, she managed to slow herself down so she did not sustain any fractures, but she did suffer very severe third-degree burns to her fingers and hands, along with several bruises and scrapes. Ray rappelled down immediately and took her to the local hospital for medical treatment. She made a very good recovery after about three weeks in bandages.

Analysis
Considering Chris' unfamiliarity with rappelling, she should have been belayed. Ray could have rappelled first and stood ready to pull the ropes to stop Chris' descent in case she lost control. Or he could have rigged a prussik on the rope as a safety device for her, or, best of all, belayed her from the top with one rope while she rappelled on the other. (Source: Harry Fischer)

FALL ON ROCK, PROTECTION PULLED OUT
Nova Scotia, Eagle's Nest, "No Man's Land"
September 30 was a great climbing day at Eagle's Nest. The cool morning air of Fall was quickly warming up, the skies were clear, and the rock was cool to the touch. It was the type of day Brian Merry dreams of for climbing, and he was on his way with two companions to try the 5.11 route on "No Man's Land" again. He had led it cleanly the previous season on fixed protection, but had a spotted record of attempts on it this year, finally getting up it on a top rope in August after a lot of falls, but he was not happy with that performance. He was feeling terrific this day, and eager to set the record straight.

First Brian rappelled down the route to inspect it, review the problems, and perfect a sequence of moves. Then he tried the climb on a top rope, and his sequence worked like a charm. High on his success, he decided immediately that he had to lead the route on natural protection, the only way he could feel he had really 'nailed' it. Even using the bolts on lead wasn't good enough. He had to have the natural lead, and the top rope went so well that he had to have it today. As he was lowered off, he picked a spot for a critical piece he would need above the crux. He measured the crack with his thumb, and knew the #7 would stick like flies on jam. At the base, he carefully prepared his rack for the most efficient place-and-clip, while his belayer Mike tried to talk him out of it. Then the top rope hit the ground, and the fear factor instantly set in, which would help him make wise decisions and keep him healthy.

Then he was off, up the crack, but about a meter before the split, he felt he should get a piece in, for no particular reason, though he felt secure and would be able to place another one a bit higher. Unfortunately, he didn't have what he needed, and had to climb down twice before he got it right—a 3.5 Friend. Right beside the first bolt, he had to choose between a bomber flexy Friend or a so-so #8 nut, and decided on the nut, as he might need the Friend a little higher up. He placed the nut, then climbed easily through the crux to the spot for the #7 DMM. With his left hand on a hold, he placed the nut, set it, then he pulled up rope and tried to clip in, but fumbled the 'biner. He tried again, missed, and felt his hand slip a bit. He needed chalk, but could not reach it, so he got a better grip on the hold and went for the clip a third time

Less than a meter below the top anchor, at 1235, his hand popped off the hold and he was on his way earthward! Out of the corner of his eye he saw his #8 nut flapping in the air. He should have used that flexy Friend after all. Strange feelings rushed through him as he realized he was about to hit. His feet hit first as the rope came tight. Then his back hit, flat on the smooth rock, and was not injured. Luckily, his head did not hit, as he had no helmet. He ended up hanging inverted at eye level to Mike, who lowered him a few more feet to a ledge. Brian's feet were obviously in bad shape, and Deborah, a nurse, cut his new climbing shoes off them, while Mike went for help. In the next three hours the Fire Department evacuated Brian, and the ambulance took him to hospital.

He had only a hairline fracture in the right foot, but his left heel was splintered, and the bone between it and the ankle was "shattered into a powder". Also the left ankle and foot had torn ligaments. After five days in hospital, he went home in two casts and a wheelchair, and is recuperating, with hopes that the broken bones will fuse and he will be able to climb again. (Source: Brian Merry)

FALL ON ROCK, INADEQUATE PROTECTION, PITON PULLED OUT
Ontario, Little Blue Mountain

On June 18, Bruce Stover (19), Sherri May (18), John Rothwell (23), Kip Brennan (15), and I (Shawn Shea, 30) arrived at Little Blue Mountain about 1:00 p.m. to do some top roping and lead climbs. Bruce was leading a 5.10 climb called "A-Okay" that he had completed on other occasions. I was belaying another lead climb 30 feet away. Bruce seemed to be moving at a steady pace and had just clipped a pin a few feet before the crux. As he was attempting to pull through the crux, his footing slipped and he fell, pulling out the pin, 45 feet to the ground, landing in between a number of large boulders. All members in our party immediately rushed to the victim's aid and found him conscious and able to communicate. Two others in an adjacent party ran ten minutes to the local O.P.P. detachment where a rescue squad was called for.

It was determined that Stover had leg and possible pelvic injuries, and so he was secured to a board and passed over the talus by the evacuation team. He was then walked out to a field beside the highway where a helicopter was waiting to transport him to the nearest hospital. He was later listed in stable condition with a broken femur and fractured pelvis.

Analysis

Bruce is a very experienced local climber, and like many other climbers in the area, routinely clips into fixed protection with an assumption that it is bombproof. Many local routes are protected by pitons and quarter-inch bolts which may be very dated and not routinely checked. Although a visual inspection of the pin would indicate that it was not very old, its placement had probably not been checked that year, and as such this should serve as a reminder: ALWAYS BACK UP FIXED GEAR.

The parties involved are grateful for the efficient evacuation, and say that since such accidents are rare in that area, it proves the effectiveness of rescue training with the local emergency units. (Source: Shawn Shea)

RAPPEL ERROR—ONLY CLIPPED INTO ONE ROPE, NO BELAY, NO HARD HAT
Ontario, Milton, Kelso Conservation Area, "Jolly Rodger" Route
Two climbers, S. H. and W. T. from Mississauga, finished climbing the route "Jolly Rodger" around 1400 on August 23, and decided to rappel down the route. S. H. would go first, but declined a safety belay which W. T. offered him. A tree was slung with a piece of webbing, the doubled rope was secured to it with two non-locking carabiners, and then S. H. clipped his descender in to the rope. But as he leaned back to start the rappel, one side of the rope slid up through the anchor carabiners, and S. H. fell some 20 meters to the ground; he had clipped in only one side of the rappel rope. Nearby climbers assisted and ran to the lifeguard station for help, and rescue personnel reached the victim within minutes, but S. H. did not revive, and was pronounced dead on arrival at the hospital at 1500.

Analysis
S. H.'s level of rappel experience is not known, so his error could have resulted from either unfamiliarity or haste. While there were easy ways down from the top, W. T. offered a safer approach to rappelling in the form of a top belay.

Every aspect of the rappel system is important and should be verified, including the harness, the clip-in, the threading of the descender, the rope, the anchor attachment, and the anchor itself, before a commitment is made. In this case, the tree may have been adequate as a single anchor, but use of two separate slings is recommended, as is the use of two locked safety carabiners or two standard carabiners with gates outward and opposite. Also, partners should thoroughly check each other's setup. Finally, S. H. did not wear a helmet, which could have saved his life. (Source: Robert Stock, Ontario Climbing Instructor)

FALL ON ROCK, PROTECTION PULLED OUT—LEADER AND BELAYER, DEHYDRATION/FATIGUE
Ontario, Bon Echo Provincial Park, "Ottawa" Route
On September 4, J. N.(47) was leading the second pitch of "Ottawa" (5.7), belayed by M. C.(22), when he fell while attempting the crux of the route. J. N. sustained a contusion to his right thigh and abrasions to his right hand. He then set up an intermediate belay stance, using two rusted fixed pitons just below the crux, one of which had just held his fall, to bring up M. C. When M. C. arrived, J. N. told him they should descend about five meters to a good crack and set up a 'state of the art' belay, but M. C. had already led that section twice that summer and said there was no reason he should fall.

M. C. took the rack, and started up the crux moves. He clipped a runner over the neck of one of the belay pitons, as its eye was used for the belay setup, then continued climbing. He placed one more piece, and then about four meters above the belay, M. C. called out, "Falling." His protection pulled out and he fell past J. N., causing a near-factor-two load on the belay. The belay anchor failed, and both climbers fell about 55 meters into Mazinaw Lake, where they sank rapidly under the weight of their gear.

M. C. sustained a broken neck on impact with the water, became unconscious, and drowned. J. N. managed to disengage himself from him, swim to the surface in overwhelming pain, and hang onto a hold until he was reached by boat. He had suffered a crushed thoracic vertebra, two broken ribs, chest compression, deformation of the spine, and strained muscles, ligaments, and tendons in his back. M. C. was recovered from the water after being submerged about ten minutes, but did not respond to efforts to revive him. Authorities were notified, and members of the ARC Toronto Section assisted in investigating the accident.

Analysis
J. N. and M. C. were climbing within their abilities, but had been at it all day when they attempted this route as a last effort. Dehydration caused by several hours of exertion at 25-30° C may have weakened them, and one of them mentioned that their last climb had taken a lot out of him. Also, it had rained the previous evening, so the route may have had slippery sections. In any case, after J. N.'s fall, his injuries were serious enough for the climbers to retreat, but they unfortunately decided to continue. Finally, J. N. used questionable anchor pitons directly below the crux moves for his intermediate belay, when a more secure stance was available at the top of a ramp to his right. The accident may have been prevented by greater caution, as any one of the following actions would have saved them: retreating after J. N.'s scrape, belaying from a reliable anchor, or placing adequate protection. Basic security should be the top priority. (Source: J. N., W. Lansing, ACC paramedic, and Robert Stock)

AVALANCHE, LOST EQUIPMENT, STRANDED
Yukon, St. Elias Mountains, Mount Logan
On July 28, a party of four climbers were involved in an avalanche at about the 4600-meter level on the East Ridge of Mt. Logan, a short distance above their camp. Although no one was seriously injured, two of them were shaken up, and they lost some climbing equipment and food. They made their way back to the camp, and were able to radio out for assistance.

The following day, a team was dispatched and dropped groceries, gear, and another radio into their camp. They felt that the current snow conditions made the route too dangerous to descend with the gear they had left, so they were evacuated by helicopter sling to the base of the mountain, and then flown out to the highway at the south end of Kluane Lake. Because of deteriorating weather and the high altitude, a thorough examination of the site of the accident was not feasible, and some of the climbers' gear was abandoned at their camp. Also, a language barrier made it difficult to determine much about the circumstances of the accident. (Source: Lloyd Freese, Park Warden, Kluane National Park Reserve)

Analysis
Mountaineers are often at some risk on multi-day routes like Mt. Logan's East Ridge, It is common for good snow conditions to become dangerous. Besides the inherent difficulty of recognizing avalanche hazard, climbers tend to be especially optimistic once they are near to their goal, and so may push their luck rather than abandon their commitment of time, money, and effort. (Source: Orvel Miskiw)

UNITED STATES

AVALANCHE
Alaska, Glacier Bay National Park, Mount Orville
Three climbers found dead April 25, on Mount Orville (10,495 feet) have been identified as Phil Kaufman (c. 30) and Patrick Simmons (c. 30), both of Seattle, and Steve Carroll (32) of South Hampton, New Hampshire. Another group of climbers found the three roped together at the base of Mount Orville, a 10,495-foot peak in Glacier Bay National Park about 100 miles southeast of Yakutat, trooper spokesman Steve Wilhelmi said.

All three were experienced climbers. Two of them had past experience climbing in Alaska. The three told the pilot who flew them into the area April 18 that they had researched the mountain in climbing journals and with climbing clubs, and believed that if they succeeded, they would be the first to reach its summit. Apparently they reached their goal and were descending Monday morning when they got caught in an avalanche at the 7,000-foot level.

Their bodies were found at the 5,000 foot level partially buried in snow at the end of an avalanche runout zone. Trooper Chuck Lamica said it was possible they fell off the steep rock face and then were buried by an avalanche, but judging by the number of avalanches in the area—he saw over 30 while flying over the area Tuesday—and the route they took, he believes an avalanche was the most likely possibility.

"You can see the path of the avalanche where they came down," he said.

The troopers knew the climbers' whereabouts because the men had been staying in touch by radio with the group of climbers that eventually found their bodies. The two groups didn't know each other but were dropped into the area around the same time, Wilhelmi said. (From an article in the *Anchorage Daily News*, April 27,1995, by S. J. Komarnitsky)

FALL INTO CREVASSE WHILE SKI MOUNTAINEERING
Alaska, Mount Wrangell-St. Elias National Park, Mount Wrangell
A party of five skiers attempting a ski-traverse of Mount Wrangell in Wrangell-St. Elias National Park were rescued April 11 by pilot Harley McMahan after a full day aerial search by McMahan and the National Park Service. The group was found ten miles west of the Long Glacier. The leader of the party, Dave Cramer of Tok, had dislocated his shoulder after falling into a crevasse on Nabesna Glacier. After rescuing the 46-year-old Cramer from the crevasse, the group decided to take a "shortcut" down the Long Glacier, across the Copper River and out to the Edgerton Highway instead of their planned route over the top of Mount Wrangell and down the Sanford Glacier to Gakona.

The other members of the party included Cramer's 19-year-old son Eric Cramer, his 16-year-old daughter Mara Cramer, both of Tok, Robert Rourke and Bob Groseclose of Fairbanks. Rourke, Groseclose and the older Cramer had all participated in the Alaska Wilderness Classic race when it traversed the Wrangell Mountains in 1988, 1989, and 1990. The three were experienced in ski-mountaineering and had completed previous trips in the area. (From an article in the *Mukluk News*, April 20, 1995.)

(Editor's Note: There is no indication as to whether the party was roped, which is a good idea in such terrain.)

FALL ON SNOW/ICE, PLACED NO PROTECTION, INADEQUATE EQUIPMENT
Alaska, Mount McKinley, West Buttress

On April 21, 1995, the "Angove-McKinley Expedition" departed from Talkeetna for the 7,200 foot base camp on Mount McKinley. United States Naval Officers Lt. Michael Angove (31) and Lt. Cmdr. Brian McKinley (37) were the third climbing team to land at the air strip on the South East Fork of the Kahiltna Glacier during the 1995 climbing season. Angove and McKinley arrived at the 14,200 foot camp on May 1. They spent the next several days acclimating and resting before moving their camp up to the 17,200 foot level on May 3. They spent the rest of the day at 17,200 feet resting before attempting the summit the following day.

At 0930 on May 4, Angove and McKinley departed for the summit with another climbing team, "Iced Triple Grande." The Grande climbing team consisted of Deborah Robertson and Rod Hancock who had been climbing the same timetable with the Angove-McKinley expedition since the 11,000 foot camp. The Iced Triple Grande expedition summited around 1900 with the Angove-McKinley expedition 30 minutes behind them. Hancock and Robertson descended and stopped at the bottom of the summit ridge to talk with Angove. Hancock and Robertson had wanded the entire route from 17,200 feet up to the summit ridge. Angove and McKinley had agreed to pull the wands on their way down. Hancock and Robertson arrived at 17,200 feet at 2330. They observed Angove and McKinley below Denali Pass several hundred feet at 2245. Angove and McKinley appeared okay and were descending without noticeable problems. Robertson described the conditions on Denali Pass as some soft snow mixed with ice at times, with a few sections at 40 to 45 degrees. The weather on summit day was nice with some broken clouds and good visibility. The temperature was estimated at 0° F, with light winds out of the west.

Angove and McKinley were descending roped together with Angove leading and ice axes in hand. Angove stated they didn't bring any pickets, ice screws or flukes with them on summit day. About 2330 at 17,800 feet, Angove felt the rope tighten and looked over his shoulder to see McKinley falling and attempting to self-arrest with his ice axe. Angove immediately attempted to self-arrest, but was pulled from his position by McKinley's body weight. McKinley at times was tumbling out of control. Angove and McKinley fell approximately 400 to 500 feet, with Angove landing in the bottom of a 30 to 40 foot crevasse at 17,400 feet. Angove remembers clipping his pack to the end of a slack rope which was tied off to McKinley. He began ascending the crevasse wall. Angove lost one of his crampons during the ascent. After reaching the lip of the crevasse, he followed the rope to McKinley. When Angove saw McKinley, he was not moving and appeared dead. He felt no pulse and there were no noticeable life signs. Angove remembers pulling his pack out of the crevasse and climbing back to 17,200 feet and getting into his tent to sleep. He awoke at 0900 and crawled into the tent of Robertson and Hancock. Angove was suffering from shock and internal chest pain. He explained to them the details of the accident and was given care for the next five days until his rescue. The Talkeetna Ranger Station had communication with Robertson and Hancock getting updates on weather and Angove's condition. The weather patterns at this time on Mount McKinley were unstable, with storms at all elevations preventing any expeditions from moving, including an NPS mountaineering patrol at 11,000 feet.

At 0615 on May 9, the NPS rescue helicopter landed at 17,200 feet after six attempts earlier in high winds. The helicopter with pilot Doug Drury and South District Ranger J. D. Swed landed several hundred feet east of Angove's location. Swed departed from the helicopter and assisted Angove to the ship.

They immediately departed to the 7,200 foot base camp and transferred Angove to a 210th rescue Pavehawk Helicopter. Angove was flown to the Elmendorf Air Force Base Hospital and diagnosed with HAPE, HACE, and intercostal damage to his muscles and cartilage. Brian McKinley's body was removed by the NPS rescue helicopter on May 18.

Analysis
Denali Pass has been the location of many mountaineering accidents since the early 1960s. All climbers are cautioned and briefed by mountaineering rangers about the risk factors found when descending Denali Pass. The National Park Service recommends carrying either pickets, ice screws, and/or flukes on Denali Pass in case protection is needed on the descent. Many expeditions carry protection to the 17,200 foot camp, but choose not to bring anchors higher due to extra weight. This is often a fatal mistake. Some expeditions ascend and descend Denali Pass with ski poles without technical difficulties, but have no way of either self-arresting or stopping another person if a fall occurs. Expeditions climbing Mount McKinley for the first time frequently underestimate Denali Pass. The angle of the slope is 40 to 45 degrees at the steepest, but due to the hard ice conditions in early season, it can be extremely difficult to self-arrest. Few expeditions have problems ascending Denali Pass, but many have epics descending it. This is due to extreme Arctic conditions—cold temperatures, blue ice, flat light, and high winds. Many climbers, after attempting to summit, are at their limits both physically and mentally during the descent to the 17,200 foot camp. Reaction time to falls can be severely impaired and delayed from hypoxia due to high altitude. The "Angove-McKinley Expedition" made a decision not to use or take protection descending Denali Pass. It is unclear what caused Brian McKinley to fall or why he failed to self-arrest. In this specific accident, the use of running protection may have prevented the 300 to 400 foot fall. (Source: Daryl Miller, Mountaineering Ranger, Denali National Park)

WEATHER, PROBABLY HYPOTHERMIA, combined with
SNOW BRIDGE COLLAPSE
Alaska, Mount McKinley, West Buttress
On May 26, the "Free at Last" expedition discovered three deceased climbers—Thomas Downey (52), Scott Hall (34), and Jimmy Hinkhouse (52)—at Windy Corner (13,300 feet). On May 23, the OSAT expedition, along with 12 other climbers, decided to abandon their climb and descend. At Windy Corner, the combined groups encountered unexpected gale force winds. All the groups, except the OSAT expedition, fully negotiated Windy Corner and bivouacked near the pass. The OSAT expedition chose to bivouac in a crevasse at Windy Corner. Since there were no survivors, the precise cause of death is unknown. There is evidence a snow bridge may have collapsed and struck the climbers, but there was no major trauma according to the medical examiner. Hypothermia is another possibility.

Analysis
One thing for sure is that the weather on May 23 was not good at 14,200 feet, and even worse at Windy Corner. Ultimately, the OSAT expedition made the decision to descend, unaware of the intense venturi effect at Windy Corner.

One scenario involves the snow bridge collapsing on the climbers. A small amount of blood was evident in the snow. Other evidence included snow blocks, and obvious instability of the bridge. One climber was wedged in the bridge. The medical examiner found no major trauma to any of the victims to support this theory.

Another theory is the climbers succumbed to hypothermia. The post mortem examination showed their testicles had drawn up into the inguinal cavity, a possible sign of hypothermia according the examiner. The weather is a strong factor in this theory. (Source: Kevin Moore, Mountaineering Ranger, Denali National Park)

ATRIAL FIBRILLATION
Alaska, Mount McKinley, West Buttress
On May 26, at 2100, old Swiss climber Dr. Paul Robadey (55) was flown from the 14,200 foot Ranger camp by the NPS helicopter to the 7,200 foot base camp. Robadey was diagnosed with atrial fibrillation by NPS VIP doctors and a cardiologist from the Alaska Regional Hospital via a phone consultation. Robadey was transferred to a fixed wing aircraft and flown to Talkeetna. (Source: Daryl Miller, Mountaineering Ranger, Denali National Park)

DEHYDRATION, HEAT EXHAUSTION
Alaska, Mount McKinley, West Buttress
On June 1, around 2330, Robert Paige (28) called 7,200 foot base camp, saying he was sick and could not stop vomiting. Base camp manager Anne Duquette told him that he should take fluids, if he could keep them down, and call back in the morning. The expedition called back in the morning and said that Paige was still vomiting and they would attempt to link up with an Army team that was at the 8,000 foot camp. On June 2 at 1200, NPS members Eric Martin and Amy Eilertsen were notified by Anne Duquette, and began skiing from the 7,200 camp to the 8,000 foot level. Ranger/medic Martin made contact with Paige at 7,800 feet at 1530 and began treatment for dehydration. He called for helicopter evacuation. Paige was evacuated to Anchorage, where he was found to be suffering from dehydration and heat exhaustion. It is believed this climber's condition was caused by lack of adequate fluids and hot weather. (Source: Daryl Miller, Mountaineering Ranger, Denali National Park)

ACUTE ABDOMEN
Alaska, Mount McKinley, West Buttress
On June 2, at 2100, Tom Bohanon of the "Three Guys on Denali" expedition came to the ranger camp at 14,200 feet complaining of hematemesis (vomiting blood). Bohanon was examined and diagnosed as having an acute upper gastrointestinal bleed. VIP's Dr. Colin Grissom and Dr. Lada Kokan assessed Bohanon's medical condition and felt it was life threatening. Bohanon was evacuated at 2315 with the NPS helicopter to Talkeetna, and was transferred to a "Flight for Life" fixed wing aircraft and flown to an Anchorage Hospital. (Source: Daryl Miller, Mountaineering Ranger, Denali National Park)

Analyses
These three illnesses reported above, all of which required costly evacuation, demonstrate the spectrum that runs from preventable to unpredictable. The dehydration and

heat exhaustion case is not uncommon—even at altitudes and in the snow environment. Those who are relatively new to glacier travel on sunny, windless days "forget" to take in adequate liquids. The atrial fibrillation case was a pre-existing condition for which the victim—a doctor at that—had medication. However, altitude may play a part in amounts and frequency of medication, and often these factors are not taken into consideration. Age can also be a factor. As for the gastrointestinal bleed—with no previous history, the reality is that sometimes acute illness strikes, no matter where we are. (Bohanon was able to be put on IV fluids, oxygen, and medication at the 14,200 foot camp—a luxury that is not always available.) Knowing one's medical history and understanding the environments to be encountered—which includes the evacuation possibilities—can reduce the potential for life threatening illness. (Source: Jed Williamson)

FALL ON SNOW, EXPOSURE, PROBABLY AMS
Alaska, Mount McKinley, West Buttress

On June 9, a Spanish climber fell 4,000 feet to his death on Mount McKinley while two of his fellow countrymen clung to a frosty perch just below the summit until they were rescued with a litter after 2300.

The death came near the end of a day of efforts to rescue the three Spaniards, including one attempt in which a Park Service helicopter nearly crashed while trying to bring the climbers down from the 19,200 foot level.

Earlier in the day, National Park Service officials had tried to reach the three men with a high-altitude helicopter, but nearly crashed after a climbing rope hit its tail rotor. The helicopter had to fly down to the base camp to await a mechanical inspection and was later grounded. With the Park Service's only chopper out of commission, U.S. Army Chinook helicopters from Fort Wainwright near Fairbanks were requested to fly to Talkeetna and stand by for a possible rescue.

Meanwhile, besides the three dropped off by helicopter, a pair of other volunteers had headed up from the 14,200 foot camp on Friday morning to see if they could climb over the summit of the mountain and descend the West Rib to reach the climbers, identified as Xavier Delgado Vives (34), Clinewt Lupon (34), and Albert Puig (26).

"We're moving the chess pieces around all over the mountain," Park spokesman Quinley said earlier in the evening.

The Spaniards were overdue as of Thursday from their attempt via the difficult West Rib, but Park Service rangers had not been particularly worried. The trio got a late start, and thus some delay was expected.

Rangers asked another group of climbers beginning an ascent of the rip to watch for the three. When spotted on Thursday, the Spanish climbers had stopped moving. The Park Service tried to talk to them by radio, but communications were difficult because none of them spoke much English.

"This morning, we talked to them through an interpreter," Quinley said. "We're still not sure what the deal is. They're not moving. They were talking about frostbite, but it's sounding more like AMS."

The Park Service's Aereospoattle Llama helicopter on Friday was able to drop the group water, an extra radio and other supplies before near-disaster struck it. After the delivery, Ranger J. D. Swed was supposed to drop a climbing rope from the helicopter.

"They got the bag," Quinley said, "but the rope caught on one of the (helicopter's skids), and they couldn't shake it loose." The helicopter tried to descend to 16,200 feet to land and cut the rope loose, but a gust of wind tossed the line over the tail boom.

"As J. D. said, several years went by in several seconds there," Quinley said. "Life on the edge, a little over the edge on that one."

It was worse for rangers on the ground. Daryl Miller at the 14,200 foot camp saw the helicopter disappear behind a ridge and thought it had gone down. So did Ranger Kevin Moore, who was flying support with pilot Jay Hudson.

"Luckily, the rotor cut the rope clean," Miller said. (Source: From an article in the *Anchorage Daily News*, by Craig Medred, David Huylen, and S. J. Komarnitsky)

Analysis

The two surviving climbers were lifted off and flown eventually to the hospital in Anchorage, where they were treated for exposure and frostbite. The exact outcome is not known. I was in Talkeetna at the time, and was told that they had been warned by other climbers to descend earlier, because it was known that the weather was going to get worse. They allegedly told these other climbers, "We will get a rescue. We have paid." The latter refers to the $150 fee that each climber on Mount McKinley is now required to pay as part of defraying the educational program for climbers, as well as the ranger camp at 14,200 feet. Foreign climbers who are used to rescue insurance are understandably interpreting the fee as being just for that purpose. (Source: J. Williamson)

FALL ON SNOW—SKI MOUNTAINEERING, AMS, WEATHER—EXTREME WINDS
Alaska, Mount Foraker, Sultana Ridge

On June 10, at 2230 Julie Faure (33), Jim Hopkins (31), John Montecucco (29), and Tyson Bradley (29) started up the Sultana Ridge on Mount Foraker (17,400 feet) from a high camp at 12,000 feet. Winds blew 25 to 30 miles per hour and the party cramponed swiftly on firm snow, reaching 14,000 feet in two hours. At 16,000 feet, the view of Denali and Hunter became obscured by a tenticular cloud forming on the summit of Foraker, and winds tripled in speed. Julie was blown off her feet several times but self-arrested immediately, and everyone continued climbing to 16,800 feet, where the route meets the broad summit plateau. John and Jim, climbing on one rope, turned around and began skiing down, citing high winds and John's possible altitude-related "off" feeling. Faure and Bradley continued toward the summit, but retreated at 17,100 feet due to unrelenting gusts up to 100 miles per hour.

Montecucco was blasted off his feet and landed on his back at 16,000 feet on the ski descent. He slid and tumbled over seracs and steep, bulletproof snow for 2,000 feet. He self-arrested with the ice hammer attached to his ski pole just one foot from a giant glacial terminus calving onto the north face of Foraker.

Hopkins skied down carefully and reached shouting distance in 15 minutes. Montecucco said he was "OK," but also said, "Who are you?" Hopkins approached the potentially overhung edge and coached his partner back from it. After accepting a down parka and what fluids he could through badly cracked lips, Montecucco became lucid and assisted greatly in his own evacuation.

Faure and Bradley skied down without incident as winds lightened, and administered pain killers within an hour of the fall. Montecucco was short roped and lowered on his slippery down pants. A ground evacuation was deemed unreasonable in light of the five miles of undulating, exposed ridge leading back to the summit of Mount Crosson. The direct descent to the Kahiltna Glacier would have been highly avalanche and ice fall prone. It had been the site of previous accidents.

A military rescue helicopter met the party at their high camp (12,000 feet) and whisked Montecucco to Talkeetna. He was diagnosed with a broken and a sprained ankle, and bruised ribs. He allowed the ankle a week to reduce in swelling, and was successfully cast in Palmer, Alaska, near his home on Lazy Mountain. He has recovered completely as of this writing, but he is taking time off from big peak ski-mountaineering. (Source: Letter from Tyson Bradley)

EXPOSURE, DEHYDRATION, INADEQUATE EQUIPMENT (Rope, Altimeter, Compass, Clothing), PARTY SEPARATED, EXCEEDING ABILITIES
Alaska, Mount McKinley, West Buttress

A group of thirteen Taiwanese were training for an Everest expedition. Twelve of the group flew into 7,200 foot base camp on May 31, with the final team member arriving on June 8. Four team members, Chang Yang-Du, Kuang Ming Wang, Chang Shun Ming, and Tyi-Hone Cheng, climbed to 17,200 feet on June 8. Chang Shun Ming and Tyi-Hone Cheng left from 17,000 feet on June 9, went to the summit, then returned to 17,000 feet, picked up the two remaining team members and left. These four team members were not involved in the rescue in any way, except in that they were part of the original group that came to climb and train on Denali.

Eight more of the party climbed to 17,000 feet, and prepared for summit bids. By June 13 they felt ready to make their summit attempt. Seven of them left 17,000 feet at 1000 on June 13. They were Makalu Gau, team leader, Chen Jung Chung, Lin Tao Ming, Chiu Jui-Lin, Wu Min Chung, Kaotien Tzu, and Shieh Tzu Sheng. One team member, Ming Chun Cheng, was sick and stayed behind at 17,000 feet. Each team member carried his own food and stove. No sleeping bags were carried. None of the team members climbing to the summit had experienced any sickness at 17,000 feet. They had good weather on the way to the summit, and all seven made the summit around 1800, where they spent less than five minutes. The temperature was approximately 1° C, the winds were calm, and bad weather began coming in just after they left the summit. A storm had moved in from near the Football Field. They couldn't see any of their wands in the poor visibility, which had dropped to fifteen feet, and the winds picked up out of the northeast, blowing 20-30 mph. The group was last seen with all seven members alive at the summit by the Royal Hong Kong Police group, who noted that the Taiwanese lacked cohesiveness, and would sit down alone without telling anyone.

They descended to 19,400 feet, where they bivouacked. They huddled together, and attempted to dig in using ice axes and their feet. They ate most of their emergency food, drank their remaining water, and attempted to make more water.

In the morning the weather had not improved. Their limbs were numb but they were not sure if they had frostbite. The group again had difficulty finding their way down. They had no map, no compass, no altimeter, and no rope. They walked in circles for a time. At some point in time that was not able to be determined, they split into two distinct groups. The first group consisted of team leader Makalu Gau, Kaotien Tzu, Chen Jung Chung, and Shieh Tzu Sheng. The second group consisted of Chiu Jui-Lin, Doin Min Lin, and Wu Min Ching. The group of four found the trail and began descending. They waved back to the other three to follow. Two of the remaining three started to follow. (These are the two who were later rescued by NPS patrol members Alex Lowe and Conrad Anker.)

The group of four got to camp at 17,000 feet on the evening of June 14. They joined up with their one team member who had waited. At this point, five of the original group were at 17,000 feet. Three were at 19,000; of these three, two were injured and one was dead in the rocks near Archdeacon's Tower. The five at the 17,000 camp tried to radio back to the remaining three, but received no answer. Several groups at 17,000 feet helped the Taiwanese with their frostbite.

Chen Jung Chung and Shieh Tgu Ching were rescued from 17,000 feet by NPS Lama on June 15 at 1235, flown to the 7,200 foot base camp, where they were stabilized. A full medical survey was done, their frostbite was evaluated, and they were questioned about the accident. They were then transported to Alaska Regional Hospital via National Guard Pavehawk.

On the morning of June 15, an aircraft from Hudson Aviation and NPS ranger Joe Reichert searched the upper mountain. They spotted two of the three climbers near the 19,400 foot level. Doin Min Lin and Wu Min Chung were assisted by NPS patrol members Alex Lowe and Conrad Anker from 19,400 feet to 17,200 feet, where they were airlifted on June 15 at 1932 to Talkeetna by an Army Chinook, then transported to Alaska Regional Hospital by National Guard Pavehawk.

Doin Min Lin and Wu Min Chung were found to be suffering from hypothermia, frostbite, and dehydration. They had not been able to take in any liquids for two days, due to their prolonged bivouac. The more critical of the two patients was Wu Ming Chung, due to severely frostbitten fingers and toes.

Chiu Jui-Lin was found dead near Archdeacon's Tower by NPS patrol member Alex Lowe. Chiu was not wearing gloves or mittens, and had on only a light outer jacket and pants. After checking for pulses and determining that Chiu's body was rigid, frozen and pulseless, Lowe secured the body for later recovery (on June 17).

All remaining members were assisted down to the 14,000 foot camp by NPS and NPS patrol members, and climbing groups.

Analysis
This accident was caused by a number of factors. A lack of skill in accurately understanding weather patterns on Denali meant that the Taiwanese missed vital clues about when the weather would change. A lack of critical route finding tools such as a map, compass, and altimeter prevented the team from navigating accurately down from the summit. Splitting the group weakened an already struggling team. A lack of sleeping bags and other bivouac gear left the team vulnerable to sudden weather changes. It is clear that this team tragically underestimated the severity of conditions on Denali. (Source: Eric Martin, Mountaineering Ranger, Denali National Park)

AVALANCHE
Alaska, Mount McKinley, South Buttress
The "South Buttress 95" expedition members included leader Tom Fitzsimmons (45), Jim Fitzsimmons (38), Richard Rodgers (40), and David Hoffman (49). Their intended route was the 1954 ascent of the South Buttress from the Ruth Glacier.

On June 16, the group was flown to the Ruth Glacier to begin their approach. They had established a base camp at the 9,200 foot level of the West Fork near the head of the cirque. Two days were spent fixing 900 feet of line and advancing supplies to approximately the 10,800 foot level, positioned in the middle of a face. This face is the start of the difficulties, comprised of 2,000 feet of snow slopes and ice bulges, with angles from 30 to 60 degrees, and having a southeast aspect. While working this lower face section, they encountered two crevasses whose uphill lips were higher than the downhill lips, forming cliffs of 40 and 100 feet. The expedition weaved around an end of the first crevasse. They climbed 600 feet higher and located a cache under the awning of the 100 foot cliff.

On June 24 and 25, a storm moved in dumping nearly two feet of snow, combined with wind gusts up to 40 mph. The group was camped at 9,200 feet during the storm. They were aware that the face they had been working was now a leeward slope in the storm, and probably being loaded, with wind transported snow. On June 26 the weather cleared creating the hottest, clearest day the group had yet experienced on this trip. Instead of climbing during this break, the expedition waited 36 hours for the slope to settle. They did not observe any avalanche activity while they waited.

On June 27 at 0230 the group began climbing the face. It was more difficult than they had anticipated. This slowed their initial progress, and combined with a two day storm, made the group a little anxious about being able to finish their climb. They were cognizant of the potential for avalanches. There were sixteen days left in their schedule for climbing. These two factors offset their anxiety somewhat.

On the climb up the face, the conditions varied between ice and pockets of snow. They linked up the ice patches to minimize the trail breaking. When they reached their cache under the 100 foot ice cliffs, they were nearly two-thirds of the way up. The sun was now again heating the face, and they realized that they hadn't left early enough to complete the face. The group decided to wait until the slope hardened again before continuing to the top. During the wait, the snow formed a breakable crust.

On June 27 at 2100, they resumed climbing as two rope teams. David and Tom led out fixing two 300 foot ropes, with Jim and Richard following behind. The slope angle was approximately 50 degrees for the two rope span, then it appeared to lay back to 30 degrees in a small bowl above, before it reached the top. The fixed ropes were anchored with seven pickets. The pickets were hammered through the snow into the ice as far as possible, which mangled the heads of the pickets. The climbers were confident in their placement. About 2300, David was at the top of the fixed lines belaying Tom as he climbed, and Jim and Richard were below them when the avalanche occurred. Tom heard a loud Whumph! and felt the slope in a 600 foot by 200 foot section give way above, below, and beneath them. Everyone and everything began moving with the slide. They began swimming and struggling to stay on top of the moving snow. The slide path was in line with the ice cliffs, and the climbers were swept over the 100 foot cliff in a cascade of debris, ropes and bodies. They impacted the angled slope below and stopped for a moment. The snow continued to pour over the cliff and began burying them. The slide regained its momentum and again pulled the climbers downhill with it. They were tossed over the second ice cliff and impacted the slope below, except for Tom who fell another 40 feet into the crevasse after failing to clear the gap. The climbers and the avalanche debris lost momentum and stopped here below the 40 foot ice cliff at 10,700 feet.

Tom hung upside down in the crevasse tangled in ropes. His injuries were a gash above the knee (which later required thirteen stitches), contusions and abrasions. Tom pulled on the ropes he was tangled in and determined the best anchored rope, and clipped a jumar into it. He then freed himself by cutting the remaining lines with a knife.

Jim and David lay unconscious above for a brief moment as Richard tried to communicate with everyone. Richard was able to contact Tom in the crevasse and soon Jim and David were conscious. Richard stood first, but later would have to lie down because of his chest injuries. David cut himself free of the ropes and went to assist Jim, who was in considerable pain and unable to free his foot, which was buried below the knee and twisted badly. The debris had set up quickly and it was difficult for David to dig Jim's foot out. David then went to the crevasse lip, and assisted Tom out of the crevasse by tying a line to his pack and hauling. Tom went to Jim and put a down coat on him, while David helped Richard lie down in a position of comfort to ease his breathing. Tom began calling on a CB radio, blindly relaying their location and that there was an emergency. The message was received by Annie Duquette at Kahiltna base camp, and a bush resident near Bald Mountain outside of Talkeetna. Between making frequent broadcasts on the radio, Tom and David were able to set up the tent, bandage Richard's chest, and administer Demerol to Jim.

AT 0020 the Park Service received the call of an emergency on the Ruth Glacier. At 0459 both patients were loaded into a Pavehawk helicopter and transported to Alaska Regional Hospital.

Analysis
The weather in the Alaska Range this season was unstable. There were many storm days resulting in loaded slopes. The South Buttress expedition, although cognizant of avalanche hazard and having taken some definite precautions, were caught in an avalanche. It is difficult to say whether waiting several more hours would have allowed the snow to bond well enough to prevent what appeared to be a wet slide. The long Alaskan day oftentimes prevents sufficient freezing of the snow pack over night. The slope may have had a long term unstable characteristic, in which case waiting several hours would have been useless. (Source: Kevin Moore, Mountaineering Ranger, Denali National Park)

(Editor's Note: On May 25, with an accumulation of seven feet of new snow in five days, a Cessna 185 flipped over on takeoff from the Kahiltna base camp.)

FALL INTO CREVASSE—SNOW BRIDGE COLLAPSE, POOR POSITION, INADEQUATE PROTECTION—NO BELAY OR FIXED ROPE
Alaska, Mount McKinley, West Buttress
On June 28 at 1900, Dominic Marshall (25) and Reggie Perrin fell into a crevasse at 13,600 feet while ascending the West Buttress. Perrin is disabled and Marshall was assisting him to walk when the two broke through a bridged crevasse. Marshall held Perrin from the surface while Perrin went in about three feet. They were extricated very quickly by their party. Perrin was unhurt while Marshall experienced a lot of pain to walk. Marshall was sledded into the 14,200 foot ranger station at 2130. Marshall complained of pain in his pelvis and lower back. A thorough exam was conducted by Canadian Rescue Medic John Oaks of the NPS patrol with assistance from Dr. Dunken Gray and Dr. Anthony Osborne of the Unseen Steps party. It was determined that Marshall should be evacuated by helicopter. Marshall's continued pain left speculation of a potential fracture of the lower pelvis. Marshall was released on June 29 with a torn pelvic cartilage.

Analysis
John Barry stated the following: "I was part of a rope of six, moving from a camp at about 12,100 feet to the plateau at 14,200 feet. The visibility was good and the weather fair. One of our party, 'Reggie' Perrin is disabled—partially paralyzed in the left arm and leg and 75% blind. This means that when moving roped on glaciated terrain, we have to configure the rope so that, whilst everyone is joined in the normal way, Reggie—who needs a shoulder adjacent his arm on all but the easiest ground—has a fellow climber immediately alongside. This I achieve by means of a doubled rope and sling.

"We were rounding a corner about 13,600 feet near the end of a pleasant but uneventful day when the rope tightened. Looking back I saw that Reggie and his helper of the day, Dominic Marshall, had fallen through the path. Marshall was only waist deep;

Perrin was about three feet into a crevasse. I organized a hoist and in ten minutes or so we had pulled them clear."

If traveling with a person who needs assistance means that normal practices have to be abandoned, then one must be prepared for the consequences—or make adjustments to the procedures. In this case, a fixed line and/or a belay may have compensated for the two climbers being side by side. (Source: Jed Williamson and Roger Robinson, Mountaineering Ranger, Denali National Park)

RAPPEL ERROR—FAILED TO THREAD BOTH ROPES THROUGH FRICTION DEVICE, NO BELAY
Arizona, Cochise Stronghold

On October 28, John Payne, Jr., Mark Plassman, and Bruce McKenzie set off for "What's My Line," a three-pitch 5.6 in Cochise Stronghold. The trio topped out in the early afternoon and had lunch. After lunch, they set up the rappel and Bruce headed down to the first ledge, a mere 30 feet down and as big as a living room. Next came Mark. John started his descent and screamed. He hadn't threaded both strands through his tuber. He fell just past the ledge, glancing off, and disappeared, taking not only the rope he was tied into with him, but also the second line which he had strapped to his back. We will never know what happened to John when he roped in—he screwed up and it cost him his life. If he had started the rap eight feet to the right, he would have had a 30 foot fall.

Bruce and Mark were left on the ledge with some extra food and some webbing. The next morning they signaled some hikers and tried to get them to do the route using John's gear; neither of them were climbers, however and the weather had become inclement: rainy and windy. The hikers left to get Search and Rescue—a six hour hike at least. After ten hours, SAR came in. It was still rainy and they were unable to get a rope to Bruce and Mark. At this point a chopper was called in. It's unclear what the original purpose of the chopper was, because after hovering for a while it left to get some rope and coats to drop to Bruce and Mark.

When the chopper returned with 200 feet of rope, Bruce and Mark had been on the ledge for over 30 hours. The rope was delivered and Bruce and Mark rapped the rest of the way down. They did have extra clothes and rain gear, but it was at the base of the climb. Both Bruce and John had done the route numerous times previously. The choice of route was made because it was known by both quite well and Bruce and Mark had never climbed together. Ironically, John did check Mark, who was using an ATC, before he rapped. (Source: Brian McKenzie)

DARKNESS—LATE START, DEHYDRATION, HYPOTHERMIA (CARRIED NO WATER), INADEQUATE CLOTHING, CREATING A HAZARDOUS CONDITION
California, Yosemite Valley, Manure Pile Buttress, Nutcracker

On March 30, at 2310, Reza Tabrizi (22) called NPS dispatch from the Camp 4 pay phone to report that his two climbing partners, Mark Bradford (23) and Sarah Rich (20), were stranded by darkness at the top of Manure Pile Buttress.

While driving back to the Manure Pile parking area with Ranger Mike Archer, Tabrizi stated the following: The three had reached the top of Nutcracker after dark, with no lights. The way down was known to be dangerous in the dark, so he had left the others on top with a rope and a rack of hardware while he rappelled alone with the other rope down the west side of the buttress. The time was about 1930. On the last rappel he had accidentally rappelled off the end of his rope, falling 20 feet to the ground, but he was not hurt.

He then got three unidentified visitors in Camp 4 to assist him with lights. However, when they arrived at Manure Pile, they found that none of their headlamps worked, and they also couldn't make voice contact with Johnson and Rich. So Tabrizi had driven back to Camp 4 and contacted the NPS. He stated that Johnson and Rich were not injured when he left them, but that they were without warm clothes, food, or water, and that Rich lacked her asthma medication. (The low temperature that night was 31° F.)

While another ranger tried to contact the party with a loudspeaker, Archer and Tabrizi hiked up the regular descent route. Just after midnight they heard Johnson answering their calls. He stated that he and Rich were on top of the climb and were unhurt but very cold, and that Rich was having difficulty breathing due to her asthma. Because of Rich's condition, Archer asked that an ambulance and additional rescuers stand by at the parking area.

Archer and Tabrizi reached Johnson and Rich at about 0020. Rich stated she was breathing more easily, but Archer requested that rangers Keith Losber and Chris Robinson (both paramedics) come to the scene to accompany Rich down. She was weak and dizzy, probably due to lack of food, so she was belayed down the descent. Everyone reached the ground without incident.

Analysis
Tabrizi and Johnston had each climbed big walls and had climbed Nutcracker previously. Rich was a novice, with no leading experience. This was her first multi-pitch climb.

They had begun climbing the route about 1330. It was near dusk by the time they reached the end of the second pitch. They had decided to continue instead of retreating, although they knew they could retreat with the equipment they had. It was completely dark by the time Johnston led the last (5th) pitch.

The party did not take water, headlamps, or warm clothes because "it was only the Nutcracker." Rich did not carry her medication, assuming she would not need it.

Tabrizi and Bradford were cited to mandatory court appearances for Disorderly Conduct/Creating a Hazardous Condition, 36 CFR 2.34 (a) (4). The NPS recommended to the court that they each pay $400, half the cost of the rescue. (Source: Mike Archer, NPS Ranger)

WEATHER, HYPOTHERMIA, INADEQUATE EQUIPMENT
California, Yosemite Valley, El Capitan, The Nose
On April 9, two parties of climbers started up the Nose (Grade VI) on El Capitan. One group included John Montecucco (30) and Shawn Kelley (28) and the other Aaron Silverman (27) and Matt Francis (25). All four had several years of experience and climbed at a high standard. All but Shawn had climbed Grade V's, and, for all, the Nose was their first Grade VI.

Each climber carried several layers of polypro, fleece, and Goretex, both top and bottom, as well as insulated socks, hats, and gloves. They had three 20-25° F synthetic bags and a 0° F down bag, three Goretex bivy sacks, and a plastic tarp. For shelter each team had brought the fly from a new A5 double portaledge, recently seam-sealed.

They fixed pitches on Sunday after checking the forecast: fair, with no storms through Thursday. On Wednesday night, the 12th, Aaron and Matt bivvied one pitch below Camp 6, while John and Shawn stopped at Camp 5. Both groups hoped to top out the next day.

Early Thursday morning it was hazy, gray, and breezy. Aaron and Matt could see it snowing across the Valley so they put on their storm clothes, then Aaron led the pitch off Camp 6 and hauled the bags. The whole way up the pitch and while waiting at the belay he was getting wet from the normal spring runoff in the corner. Matt was half-way up the pitch, cleaning, when they were hit by heavy rain and snow. They retreated to Camp 6, leaving their ropes in place, and set up their shelter.

That morning, on Camp 5, the wind had caught John's sleeping bag and had blown it away. He and Shawn nevertheless decided to continue and climbed the next pitch. The two groups decided to join forces and use all of their ropes to fix to the top, so Aaron and Matt tossed John and Shawn a line. By the time they were all together the rain was very heavy, and water was pouring down the wall and beginning to freeze. It was obvious they weren't going anywhere, so John and Shawn also set up their shelter. It was now about 1030.

Condensation built up as soon as they got under their flies. The flies were clipped to fairly high anchors but, without ledge frames to stretch them out, it was difficult to keep them off their bags and clothes so they constantly got wet. When a blast of wind and rain hit them, it knocked more condensation onto them.

John and Shawn felt that the rain and runoff was being blown straight through the fabric of their fly and that it dripped through where it pooled in low spots, but not at the seams. Water also seemed to enter via the anchor sling in the apex of the fly, soaking their daisy chains, and it ran under the fly, along the rock where their backup anchor rope lay.

They dealt with the water as best they could by arranging their pads, tarp, and clothing to shunt most of it away; John remained comfortable but Shawn had trouble keeping water out of his bivy sack, and he became soaked and hypothermic as the day progressed. It was very difficult, if not impossible, to stay dry with the gear they had and with the constantly dripping condensation and leakage. Furthermore, the rock ledge sloped a bit so they frequently had to reposition themselves with respect to the fly.

Matt and Aaron had similar problems with condensation but none with leakage. However, while Matt stayed warm and dry, Aaron, already wet from leading the pitch above, got even wetter and was soon shivering.

By late afternoon Shawn and Aaron had deteriorated further. It was obvious that going up or down on their own was out of the question. The temperature was dropping and more ice was building up on the wall and beginning to coat the inside of the flies. Shawn and Aaron felt that, for them, rescue was the only option, and their partners agreed.

At 1900 they began flashing lights at the cars below. Eventually the NPS called back with a loudspeaker and learned their situation. Flying rescuers to the Summit was not possible because it was so late in the day and the cliff was socked in, so the rangers told them not to expect help until the next morning.

John and Matt spent most of the night trying to keep their partners awake and moving, to stay warm. At 2300 John and Shawn brought out their one sleeping bag, which they'd held in reserve, and put it over both of them. In John's opinion, it slowed Shawn's deterioration significantly.

Twenty rescuers tried to get to the summit that night by taking snowcats up the Tioga and Tamarack Flat roads, then hiking the remaining eight miles. They never even made it to the trailhead—visibility was zero and the machines bogged down in one of the deepest winter snowpacks in recent memory.

Fortunately, the storm broke by midnight, allowing the team to fly the next morning and lower rescuers 600 feet to Camp 6. By 1400 all four climbers had managed to jumar to the rim. Their ascent was very difficult because of their condition and because the ropes were icing rapidly from water dripping in freezing temperatures. Just as the last rescuers were flown from the summit the clouds closed in again. For the next several days, conditions on the cliff remained windy and often below freezing, yet with water running everywhere.

Analysis
Climbing in cold, wet conditions played a key role in this and many previous cases. Once you are wet you can't dry out unless you have a complete change of clothes. Aaron said, "I would have been 100% better off had I not led the pitch out of Camp 6."

Plenty of parties successfully rely on tarps, bivy sacks, and portaledge flies, but these are much riskier than a complete portaledge because you can't depend on being in the right place to set up, and water will find many ways inside.

Opinions remain divided on the security of portaledge flies. Several climbers have claimed new, seamsealed flies have leaked. A5 thinks it is actually due to condensation and/or poor seamsealing, but Fish Products states that the fabric used in most flies is not completely waterproof. Fish recommends applying NikWax Watershed for additional protection. Seam Grip is currently recommended for seams. Whatever your solutions, test your gear before the climb.

All four sleeping bags were inadequate for El Cap conditions. Down is well known to be useless when it's wet. If Shawn's bag stayed dry it's because they didn't use it at all until after he got cold enough to need a rescue. Synthetics retain more loft but if you and the bag are wet you will need a much warmer model. Keep critical items like these clipped in. John did OK without his sleeping bag, but losing it cut their margin of safety, and that bag would have made a difference for Shawn.

Aaron and Matt had only one foam pad; they left it in the haul bag because "it was a pain to constantly take it out." Pads are critical items—take them, use them, and clip them in. (Source: John Dill, NPS Ranger)

RAPPEL ERROR—ANCHOR SLING CAME OFF, INADEQUATE PROTECTION, FALL ON ROCK
California, Yosemite Valley, Sentinel Rock.
On April 17, Charles Comstock (34) and Jay Schifferdecker (27) hiked up the third-class approach ramps to the Chouinard-Herbert route on Sentinel Rock. When they reached the climb it was late. They decided they didn't feel like doing that route after all, so they descended the same way they'd come up. The ramps had been covered with verglas earlier, and they were still wet, loose, and slippery, so the pair decided to rappel a shallow gully in the middle of the face.

Their fifth rappel anchor, two pitches above the ground, was a pointed horn, around which they looped a sling. They worried that their weight might cause the sling to pop off the horn but, after some discussion, decided it would be OK. Comstock held the sling in place on top of the horn while Schifferdecker, keeping downward pressure on it from below, eased himself into the rappel. The sling shifted while he descended, but he made it to the next anchor.

Comstock felt the sling would have come off if he hadn't stabilized it. Nevertheless, he thought he could rappel safely by himself, by staying closer to the rock at the start than Schifferdecker had.

Comstock had rappelled about 12 feet when he felt and saw the sling suddenly shift halfway off the horn and stop. He was reaching for a nearby handhold when the sling came all the way off. He fell 20-30 feet down a chimney and landed on a small ledge.

He immediately knew he was injured. Both his ankles and his right hip hurt and he could not bear weight on his legs. The anchor sling lay nearby, still around the rope, so he retied it around a nearby chockstone and rappelled/slithered on his good side down to Schifferdecker. From there he was able to rappel the final pitch to the ground, where he waited while Schifferdecker went for help.

Schifferdecker reported to the NPS at about 1400, and the first rescuers reached Comstock about an hour later. He was packaged in a full-body vacuum splint and carried a mile down to the road. X-rays at the clinic showed fractures of the right side of his pelvis, the left ankle, and both heels.

Analysis
Comstock had been climbing frequently for 16 years and led 5.9. For the last ten years he had averaged 40 expedition days/year. Schifferdecker had been climbing for 8 years and led 5.9-5.10.

Both climbers agree that the compression force of the loaded sling slid it off the point of the horn. They feel that a longer sling would have stayed in place since those forces would have been less. (Source: John Dill, NPS Ranger)

STRANDED, MISPERCEPTION—ROUTE RESEARCH, INADEQUATE EQUIPMENT, CREATING A HAZARDOUS CONDITION
California, Yosemite Valley, El Capitan Zodiac
On Sunday, June 10, Dan McOmber (26) and Curt Chesney (25) fixed three pitches on the Zodiac (Grade VI) on El Capitan, and checked the forecast—clear and mild through Thursday. They started up for good on Monday, planning to summit late Wednesday and looking forward to good weather the whole way.

This was Dan's first trip to Yosemite, although he'd climbed long routes elsewhere. For the Zodiac he brought one layer of fleece tops and bottoms, Goretex bibs and jacket, a pile hat, uninsulated gloves and socks, a Goretex bivy sack, a -20° F down sleeping bag with nylon shell, and a Fish portaledge with a 4-season fly.

Curt had climbed the Zodiac two years before and several long routes elsewhere, including mountaineering routes in winter. He brought one layer of expedition-weight fleece, Goretex jacket and pants, fingerless hunting gloves, cotton socks, no hat but the hood on his jacket, a Goretex bivy sack, and a +20° F synthetic sleeping bag. His ledge was an A5.

Each brought a Grade VI haulbag and five days of food and water, but they left their foam pads behind.

The bags were heavy and the hauling on Monday took longer than expected. A party fixing behind them on Sunday caught them and passed—with permission—costing them more time. By Tuesday night Dan and Curt had finished nine pitches, leaving seven to go and putting them behind schedule.

Wednesday was cloudy and much colder, forcing them into long pants for the first time. Curt had caught a cold; he was shivering and feeling miserable. Although they no longer expected to finish that day, they still hoped to get within a couple of pitches of the top. Nevertheless the going was slow, and they had managed just two pitches when they got hit with wind and rain in the afternoon. After finishing the Zorro roofs they set up their bivy in the rain and stopped climbing early. As one put it, "I was paranoid about being half-way through a lead and not being able to get back down in time to stay dry if it opened up." They had a fairly comfortable bivy.

Earlier that day they had watched parties bailing from other routes. With the weather so threatening, Dan and Curt were worried. They didn't think they could rappel the Zodiac, had no cheater stick or bolt kit, and figured they were committed.

The weather improved that night but looked bad again Thursday morning, and they knew they had to move fast if they were going to get off. It was raining by the time Dan started up the 13th pitch, to Peanut Ledge.

Dan: "I was in my Goretex. I was getting a bit wet but nothing major, and I was warm enough. Halfway up the pitch was a funnel with a waterfall. I thought if I climbed through it the belay would be sheltered. But the water ran down my sleeves and I got soaked and cold, to the point that no amount of will power could have gotten me up that pitch. I didn't even know if I would be able to get back down to the belay. I was so miserable I just wanted to stay right there.

"I got lowered and we set up our ledges in a hurry. It was hard, desperate, because the ledges were smacking into each other and getting tangled, and because I was so cold. I was kind of panicking at that point and wasn't as careful as I should have been. I'd been climbing with everything on and was wet through to the skin. I've never been so cold as I was then—I couldn't use my hands to work with knots. I got into my bag with all my wet clothes and my shoes on, just trying to warm up in a hurry. I knew it wasn't the best thing to do but there was no possible way I could undo my shoelaces and take my clothes off—I didn't have the dexterity. So my clothes got the inside of my bag terribly wet.

"That's when the wind really hit. On one side of the fly there's a drawstring; in the wind it was worthless. I had the cord pulled in and wrapped around my hand. The wind was lifting my ledge off the ground and slamming it back and I couldn't hold on to my fly. It would rip up and I kept getting colder and colder.

"Everything meant to be waterproof was taped or seamsealed, including the fly. It had only had four or five nights of use and had been in a stuff sack the last six months. This time, in the rain, I could see splotches on the fly, as if it had de-laminated. Big drops would hit these areas and come right through, but roll off other places like they were supposed to.

"Water was coming through to the point that I had a puddle in the bottom of my ledge. I tried to brush it out with my hands but I had to hold on to my fly. I thought about poking holes in the floor to let it drain but thought the ledge would rip apart. I also considered tipping the suspension to drain the water but didn't want to, the way the wind was knocking me around.

"A big gust would come up; I'd be holding on to keep my ledge steady and my sleeping bag would come down from around my shoulders into the pool of water. So water would get inside the bag continuously, even with the bivy sack. I was soaked to the bone, had nothing dry to put on, just getting colder and colder." Curt: "I had no leaks—my ledge was dry—but I just couldn't get warm. All I could do was lay in my bag with the hood tight and the bivy sack closed. I had bought a shorter sleeping bag to keep the weight down; I ended up ripping out the shoulders trying to move around. I had stuff sacks, knee pads, shoes, as much stuff under me as I could get. I couldn't lie on the ropes because they were soaked. I knew I was dehydrated and hadn't eaten all day, but to eat I had to get out of the fly and dig in the haul bag. It was too cold and I just wanted to lay there and shiver."

They talked about their options. Even if it was sunny on Friday, the pitch above would remain impassable from runoff. If they ever did make it to the top they'd still have to negotiate the East Ledges, while even weaker than they were now.

They debated whether and when they should call for help. They were close to the top and still physically able to jumar out, but Curt felt he might be incapable of moving by the next day; the longer they waited the more complicated and uncertain a rescue would become. Neither wanted to say the R-word, but Curt finally said, "I don't know if I can make it. Let's just call."

About 1530 they yelled down to a climber walking along the base. Although the forecast was bad and the rescue team was looking at a long hike and a stormy rescue the next day, the weather broke at 1830. They were able to fly to the top of the route and lower a rescuer 400 feet to the bivy. Dan and Curt were on top by 2000.

Analysis

Being held up by other parties, climbing more slowly than expected, and an "unpredicted storm" with rain, cold, wind, and waterfalls are all common occurrences.

Suggestions. Check all your equipment thoroughly before the climb and don't go up with anything substandard. Dan made sure the seams of his fly were sealed, but simply assumed the fabric was OK since it was fairly new. He feels the coating may have been defective. After the climb it was peeling off like a snake shedding its skin. He's not sure he would have noticed it in a preflight inspection, but certainly a forced bivy is not the place to find out. Defective materials occasionally get into even the most carefully made products, so be alert.

Carry a cheater stick and bolt kit, and find out what it takes to back off your particular route. The Zodiac has been reversed from at least the ninth pitch. Dan and Curt had read this only a month or two before but had forgotten it.

Carry enough insulation for sitting still, while wet, in sub-freezing temperatures. This means all-synthetic clothes and sleeping bags, rated for at least 0° F when dry. A single layer of fleece under Goretex is inadequate even if you are completely dry, as Curt discovered.

Foam pads are important in any cold bivy, but more so in a portaledge, because cold air is blowing directly up underneath you. They would have made a big difference for Dan and Curt, but "our Grade VI bags were completely full and we thought this was ridiculous—it looked like we were doing a two-week route. We didn't want to look like gomers, so out came the pads."

Unless you're wearing a swimmer's dry-suit, or you're sure you can get off, don't try climbing in cold rain or waterfalls. Dan may have been able to ride out the storm if he'd gone under cover while he was still dry, even with that fly and his limited insulation.

Take seriously what you read. The conditions described are real, and every mistake has been clearly articulated in print several times (see below), yet almost every hypothermic climber we've rescued in the last few years has ignored the advice. Dan and Curt had read everything, "But when we were packing in the meadow and it was 80° F, some famous big-wall ace could have come up and said, 'Take your damn coat, take your foam pad...', and I'd have said, 'Get out of my way, I've got a wall to climb.'"

Do not depend on a rescue. Only a lucky break in the weather got Dan and Curt off that night. And don't let the brief description of the rescue downplay the expense, risk, and difficulty involved.

Dan: "I'd said before, 'I'm never going to get rescued. I'm not going to put anyone else's life in danger just to save my sorry ass.' It was easy to talk the talk, but when the chips were down, we were just scared to death."

Dan and Curt were found guilty of disorderly conduct (creating a hazardous condition for themselves and others) 36CFR 2.34 (a) (4), and ordered by the court to pay $500 each to the park's rescue fund.

FALL ON ROCK, HASTE—TRYING TO STICK TO A SCHEDULE
California, Yosemite Valley, North Dome Gulley

On July 6, Dave Bedell (34) and Matt Niswonger finished climbing the South Face of Washington Column and bivouacked on the summit. Early the next morning they headed for North Dome Gulley. Bedell had descended this way previously, staying close to the Column and making several rappels. They were late for a meeting this morning so, after a couple of rappels, they decided to walk further east along a ledge system in hopes it would be faster.

They soon came to a steep, smooth, granite water course several feet wide. Niswonger climbed up 100 feet or so to a less precarious crossing. Only thin streaks of water coated the rock, so Bedell figured he could cross right where he was, without a rope, by stepping in the dry spots.

Somehow he slipped, went down, and started sliding. After about 100 feet, he went over a 15-20 foot drop and landed on his butt in a shallow depression that stopped his fall. He had tried to lead with his feet the whole way, but he was nevertheless knocked out when he hit. He regained consciousness about ten minutes later, just as Niswonger reached him. Sharp pains ran down his back and legs. His legs tingled, and it hurt to breathe.

Niswonger found his way down to the phone at Mirror Lake and contacted the Park Service at 0900. Two rangers helirappelled to the scene at about 1000, and a ground team arrived shortly thereafter. They immobilized Bedell in a vacuum body splint, gave him oxygen, and shorthauled him under the park helicopter to the Yosemite Clinic. He was then flown by AirMed to Doctor's Medical Center in Modesto, where he was diagnosed with compression fractures of vertabrae L1 and T12, as well as fractures of the right 11th and 12th ribs and several deep bruises. He has made a full recovery.

Analysis

Although you can go a number of ways, the common route down North Dome Gulley follows a trail (make that a goat path) that traverses fairly high—but below the rim—and crosses the water course well above where Bedell fell. In dry conditions no rope work is necessary.

It is interesting to note that several years ago, another climber died at the same spot trying to cross the water course at night by matchlight. (Source: Cam Sholly, John Dill, NPS Rangers)

FALL ON ROCK, EXCEEDING ABILITIES
California, Yosemite Valley, Nutcracker

On July 1, Paul Bennett (41) and Randy Kanta were climbing the Nutcracker, 5.8, on Manure Pile Buttress. Bennett led the last pitch; he climbed the low-angle slab off the belay, placed a nut in the steep corner, then climbed to the mantle, where he fell.

His protection held, but he struck the slab ten feet below feet first. The moment he hit he felt his ankle go. He tumbled over, stopped upside down, and when he looked up he saw that his ankle was bent 90° to the side.

Bennett and Kanta splinted the ankle with tape, and a nearby party tried to help lower him to the base, but after an hour of this they had gone only 30 feet. Meanwhile someone had alerted the NPS; a rescue team hiked to the top of the buttress and lowered a rescuer to the scene. Bennett was able to hop down the face to the ground, supported by the rescuer and the team's ropes. His ankle, broken in three places, required surgery.

Analysis

Bennett had been climbing off and on for ten years and could top-rope 5.10-5.11. But 5.8 was his leading limit and he had not been climbing regularly right before his Yosemite trip.

The mantle on Nutcracker, and the moves that follow, is the scene of at least one broken ankle per year. Maybe it's because the climber, concentrating on the steep corner, forgets to protect against striking the lower-angle slab below. For example, Bennett thought he was well protected and expected no consequences as he started to fall. The placements are there, if you want to avoid the same fate. (Source: John Dill, NPS Ranger)

RAPPEL FAILURE—INADEQUATE ANCHOR EQUIPMENT, NO HARD HAT
California, Yosemite Valley, El Capitan

About 1800 on July 31, Ik Tae Choi (23) died in a fall on the East Ledges descent route on El Capitan. Choi led 5.11, A3 and had six years climbing experience, including the Matterhorn, the Eiger North Face and the West Face of the Dru. On this, his first trip to Yosemite, he had climbed the Prow, and he was descending from a successful ascent of the Nose at the time of the accident. The other members of this Korean party were Sang Jun Jung (23) Yeon Soo Park (34) and Myong Hoon Kim (18). Jung and Park were experienced climbers, while this was Kim's first year.

There are several variations to the East Ledges descent. Choi's group followed one requiring three 150-foot rappels: 1) down a low-angle face, past a ledge with a live oak tree and several blocks, to a sloping ledge with bolts, 2) to a large, tree-covered pedestal, and 3) to the ground.

Park and Kim had completed all three rappels at the time of the accident, and Jung was about half-way down the second. Choi was on the sloping ledge at the top of the second, lowering the team's haulbag. The bag was six to ten feet above Jung, when Choi called down that the haul bag's rope was stuck above him, in the blocks on the first rappel. About ten seconds later, Jung saw the haul bag drop ten to fifteen feet and stop. A couple of seconds later Choi fell past him, landing on the ledge at the base of the second rappel.

Jung finished his rappel, disentangled Choi from a tree, and pulled him to a flat spot. Park came up the lines from the ground, saw that Choi was unconscious and seriously injured, and sent Kim and then Jung for help. Kim reported the accident to the park dispatcher at 1900.

Choi was bleeding from the mouth; when Park turned him over to allow the blood to drain, he saw a large wound on the back of his head. Choi was not wearing his helmet, having given it to Kim to use on the descent.

Ranger Chris Robinson, a paramedic, ascended the rappel line to Choi at about 2030. Based on his radio report, the clinic staff pronounced Choi dead at 2045.

The next morning Choi's body was removed from the scene by helicopter sling-load, and rescue team members Steve Yu and Lance Allred inspected the rappel route.

Analysis

Allred and Yu found no clues to the accident above or below the ledge from which Choi had apparently fallen, but at the ledge they found the following: A quick-draw was clipped to the anchor. Attached to the quick-draw were 1) a sling with a loop tied in the free end, apparently Choi's tie-in, and 2) a friction device (brand unknown), through which the haul line was rigged. Both ends of the haul line hung down the face. The haul bag hung from one end; the other end was free but the two ends were twisted around each other. When Yu and Allred untwisted the rope it began feeding easily through the friction device, lowering the bag.

Two of the three carabiners in the belay chain were non-locking types. The third was a locker, but was unlocked. None were doubled for security. There was no carabiner in the free end of the sling. Choi had probably anchored himself by clipping the free end of this sling to a carabiner in his harness. Jung later stated that he had found only a single non-locking carabiner in Choi's harness after the fall.

Apparently Choi managed to free the stuck haul line, and the suddenly slack rope allowed the bag to drop a short distance until the rope twisted around itself. We don't know why Choi fell, but he fell the whole pitch because either 1) he had deliberately disconnected from his anchor sling to work on the stuck rope, or 2) the sling had accidently unclipped from his harness.

Whether or not the latter occurred, Choi had set himself up for an accident by relying on four separate unlocked carabiners. The belay chain should always use locked carabiners or reversed and opposed non-locking carabiners. Furthermore, by girth-hitching the anchor sling to the harness, one carabiner can be eliminated.

The stuck rope did not cause the accident but, like some past cases, it may have led to impatience and shortcuts in safety. The tree and blocks on the first rappel are easily recognized as traps for a pulled rappel line; many climbers break that rappel into two for that reason. We never learned why the party did not pull the haul line before all members were past the potential snags. Possibly they had used it as a rappel line. (Source: Mark Harvey, Steve Yu, John Dill, NPS Rangers)

STRANDED, DARKNESS—LATE START, OFF ROUTE, INADEQUATE CLOTHING, CREATING A HAZARDOUS CONDITION
California, Yosemite Valley, Fairview Dome
On August 9, about 1100, Bill Ott (47) and Hugo Orellana (24) began climbing the Regular Route (III-IV 5.9) on Fairview Dome. They were the last party to start up the climb that day. At least five parties were already on the route so Ott and Orellana had waited about an hour for their turn.

They were slowed by the groups above, and they also had trouble placing protection. On the sixth pitch, off Crescent Ledge, they lost the route. They rappelled back to Crescent Ledge and searched for bolt anchors that they remembered being shown in the guide book as a rappel route, but they were unable to locate them. During this time it became dark; they reclimbed the off-route pitch above the ledge but had to stop there because they were lost and could no longer see to climb.

Another climbing party reported to the NPS that Ott and Orellana might need help, and at 2130 a ranger contacted them by loudspeaker. At first they denied needing assistance, by signalling with a camera flash. After a brief discussion they signalled that they did need help. They stated that a cold wind was blowing.

A ten-person rescue team started hiking at 2230 and reached the top of the route at 0017. Two rescuers went over the edge at 0130 and reached the climbers, 500 feet below, at 0200. Everyone was safely on top by 0530. Ott and Orellana were cold and exhausted. They were given food and warm drinks and assisted to the Tioga Rd.

Analysis

Orellana was dressed in climbing tights and a T-shirt. Ott was wearing shorts and a short-sleeved shirt. Neither climber had additional clothing for low night-time temperatures or a change in the weather, nor had they brought a watch or headlamps. They had studied the route topo but had left it in the car, and had brought water but no food. They had two ropes and a large rack of hardware—several full sets of nuts and cams.

The Regular Route, on the north face of Fairview, is approximately 800 feet high, involving eight pitches of 5th class and three pitches of 4th class climbing. This makes it one of the longest routes in the Tuolumne Meadows area, a serious undertaking that may require most of a day. Since the altitude of Fairview Dome lies between 8800 and 9700 feet, temperatures frequently drop below freezing at night. (The low on August 10 was 34° F and the wind chill was much lower.)

Orellana had been climbing five years and leading for three. He had climbed at other areas, including one route on El Capitan. Ott was a novice, having very limited experience since taking a four-day course the year before.

On the day prior to attempting Fairview, they had completed two one-pitch climbs and a four-pitch climb, in the Tuolumne Meadows area, which gave them the confidence to tackle Fairview. Those routes, however, are much easier and far less committing than the Regular Route.

Ott and Orellana recklessly created a hazardous condition for themselves by starting the climb at a late hour and chosing to climb into the evening when they did not have headlamps. Their clothing was inadequate for the length of the climb and the possibility of spending the night on the route, and they had all the gear they needed to rappel the route before dark. Ott and Orellana were cited for Disorderly Conduct (creating a hazardous condition), 36CFR 2.34 (A) (4). They were each ordered by the court to pay half the cost of the rescue—$990 apiece. (Source: Dave Page, NPS Ranger.)

FALL ON ROCK, NO HARD HAT
California, Yosemite Valley, El Capitan

On August 16, about noon, Brian Biega (23) was leading the 6th pitch of the Salathe Wall, belayed by Andreas Zegers (24). Their goal was to make Mammoth Terrace in two hours. They had 40 minutes to go, and Biega, nearing the end of the slab section, was "French-freeing," i.e. grabbing fixed pieces as handholds rather than free-climbing or using etriers.

Suddenly Biega called, "Watch me," and fell. Zegers saw the rope catch behind his leg, flipping him over. Biega fell backwards, headfirst, struck his head and stopped. He was unconscious and bleeding from the back of his head. He had fallen about 20 feet and was now hanging 30 feet above and 15 feet to one side of the belay.

Zegers yelled for help, then lowered Biega on the belay line and pulled him to the anchor with the haul line. He bandaged Biega's head wound and checked his vital signs: he was still unconscious, his pulse was rapid and weak and his breathing was shallow, so Zegers worried that he might be in shock from blood loss.

They had passed a large team of Japanese climbers a couple of pitches below, and now several of them came up to help Zegers lower Biega five pitches to the ground. At about this time Biega regained consciousness, although he remained confused and vomited several times during the descent. They reached the ground at 1320.

Meanwhile one of the Japanese climbers had rappelled off the climb and notified the NPS. A ground team, the park helicopter, and a medical evacuation helicopter from Modesto all responded immediately. The ground team reached the base of the wall just after Biega did and found him conscious but disoriented. Given the likelihood of a serious head injury, he was given oxygen, immobilized, and shorthauled by the park aircraft to El Cap Meadow. About 1440 he was flown to Modesto by the Medi-Flite helicopter. Biega had suffered a skull fracture but he has recovered completely except for a large gap in his memory. He remembers grabbing a copperhead and clipping a piton driven upward, but little else until he woke up in the hospital.

PROTECTION PULLED, FALL ON ROCK, INADEQUATE PROTECTION, NO HARD HAT
California, Yosemite Valley, El Capitan

While Biega was being rescued (see previous account), Kirk Bland (33), Luc Mailloux, and Kevin McCracken (23) were fixing pitches on Mescalito, several hundred yards to the east. The second pitch, A2, was Bland's lead. Just before reaching the belay he placed a birdbeak on top of a deadhead (the broken remnant of a fixed copperhead). As he reached for the anchor the deadhead blew out. The last fifty feet of the pitch had been completely fixed with copperheads and, since he rarely trusted such placements, he had not clipped the rope to any of them. He fell at least 100 feet.

McCracken looked up just in time to see Bland fall backwards and upside down, striking his head on the rock. Mailloux, the belayer, was pulled upward ten feet as he stopped the fall. Bland hung there unconscious, as blood poured down the rock from a head wound.

They called to a climber at the base to go for help. Then they lowered Bland about 20 feet and pulled him over to the belay. He regained consciousness at that time. McCracken clipped himself to Bland, and Mailloux lowered both of them to the ground. Other climbers provided a first aid kit to bandage Bland's headwound while they waited for help.

The NPS team had just driven away from El Cap Meadow after Biega's rescue when they got word of the Mescalito accident. They circled back to the trailhead and headed to the scene. The situation was identical to the previous incident and so were their actions: Bland was immobilized in case of spinal injury, given oxygen and an IV, shorthauled to El Cap Meadow by the park helicopter, and flown by medivac helicopter to a hospital in Modesto.

Bland suffered a scalp laceration and a concussion. Like Biega, he remembers nothing of the fall.

Analysis

Biega and Bland were both experienced wall climbers. Neither was wearing a helmet, but they do now. Also, Bland now clips every piece in sight! (Zegers later told Bland that his favorite method for cleaning deadheads is to weight them with a birdbeak.)

The self-rescue dilemma: Good work by several climbers made for a fast rescue in each case. Had either victim suffered from serious intracranial bleeding—where time is critical—their actions could have saved his life. However there is always danger in moving a patient suffering from trauma, e.g., the motion may cause spinal cord injury from an unstable broken neck or back, or increased bleeding in damaged organs. Whether to move or stay is often a hard call, but training in wilderness medicine will better prepare you to make the decision and to minimize the risk. (Source: John Dill, NPS Ranger)

STRANDED—ROPES JAMMED, HASTE—TO TRY TO CATCH THIEVES, INADEQUATE EQUIPMENT—NO KNIFE
California, Yosemite Valley, Middle Cathedral Rock

On September 13, Chris Heck (39) and Michael Taylor (28) set out to climb the Central Pillar of Frenzy on Middle Cathedral Rock. In Heck's words, "We had planned to do five pitches and descend the route but started down after four, after my climbing partner alerted me to the fact that someone was rifling through our packs at the base. We were in a hurry to get down and see what had been stolen, but we realized we needed to step back, slow down, and not do anything stupid."

"At the third pitch belay station, we butterflied the ropes and very carefully threw them right into the crack! Of course they were stuck. (The third pitch follows a wide, low-angle crack, a classic rope-eater) Michael rappelled with a prusik and worked to free them for an hour. He came back up for water and headed back down again for about another hour. If we'd had a knife we could have cut the rope and continued rappelling with the leftover piece. After about two and a half hours of trying to free them we shouted for help."

Someone alerted the NPS. Two rescue team members climbed to Heck and Taylor so they could rappel off. (Source: Chris Robinson, NPS Ranger and Chris Heck.)

(Editor's Note: There was no indication as to whether the vandals were successful. It reminds us of yet another dimension the increase in numbers has brought to the cimbing scene.)

FALL ON ICE, INADEQUATE BELAY
California, Temple Crag

On October 4, Gary Niblock, Mike Nichols (both 48) and Mark Harris (42) were climbing an ice chute northwest of Temple Crag. About 1300, Harris reached the top first and began watching his friends climb to the top.

Niblock and Nichols were roped together as they climbed. One of the two lost his footing and slid down the ice. The partner tried to stop the fall but was also pulled down the slope. The pair tumbled and slid an estimated 800 to 1,200 feet before coming to rest on the icy slope.

Harris climbed back down to help, tying his friends to temporary anchors to keep them from sliding further. Both men were seriously injured. Harris covered his friends with sleeping bags and hiked out for help.

Harris reached Glacier Lodge in Big Pine Canyon at 1600 and alerted the sheriff's office. Because of the seriousness of the injuries and the lateness of the day, a rescue team was immediately dispatched.

U.S. Forest Service helicopter 525 flew Nixon, rescuer Arnie Peterson and paramedic Judd Symons to the location and lowered them to a rock outcropping above the victims just before dark. The trio rappelled down, traversed the ice slope and finally reached the victims around 1900.

Nixon said both men were hypothermic and had major cuts, abrasions, and bruises.

Additionally, Niblock suffered from a broken leg and Nichols from a broken arm and ribs.

Rescuers set lines and spent the next five hours moving the pair off the ice to a sheltered rock area about 75 yards to the north. By 0100, both men were stabilized, fairly warm, and had taken some warm fluids.

At 0800 the next morning, Helicopter 525 dropped a litter and technical climbing gear at the scene, then shuttled in additional rescue personnel from China Lake Mountain Rescue. Ice and rock anchors were set and the victims lowered down the last half mile of the ice chute. By 1415 the victims were airlifted to the Bishop Airport. From there they were transported to the Northern Inyo Hospital by ambulance for treatment. (Source: From a newspaper clipping sent in without name/date.)

EQUIPMENT FAILURE—WIRED NUT BROKE, FALL ON ROCK, PROTECTION PULLED
California, Yosemite Valley, El Capitan

On October 6, about 1900, Baek Man (27) was leading the pitch off Camp 5 on the Nose, using aid. He had placed a few pieces of protection and was standing on a fixed wired nut when it broke. A small Friend he had placed pulled out during his fall, and he landed hard on Camp 5, 15 feet below.

Baek and his partner, Min Yeon Sik (30) spent the night at Camp 5 and, for unknown reasons, did not yell for help until 0700 the next day. They indicated that Man was complaining of mid-back pain. The NPS rescue team flew to the summit and lowered a ranger-paramedic 900 feet to the scene. He immobilized Man in a vacuum body splint and litter. Because of the back pain and the long haul to the summit, Man was hoisted directly from Camp 5 by the helicopter from Naval Air Station Lemoore, with a Navy medic as the litter attendant. Man's spine was not fractured, but he did have ankle and wrist fractures. He was released from the Yosemite Clinic that day.

Both climbers have ten years of climbing experience, and both were wearing helmets. (Source: Lane Baker, John Dill, NPS Rangers)

SLIDE/FALL ON ICE, INEXPERIENCE, IMPROPER USE OF CRAMPONS, INADEQUATE PROTECTION—UNCLIPPED, PARTY SEPARATED
California, Eastern Sierras, Lamarck Col

On October 22, David Lown (29), a second year family practice resident, and three friends were descending a frozen snow slope below the Lamarck Col plateau. A series of rappels were to be set up with ice bollards for the rappels and ice screws for backup and safety anchors for those waiting to rappel. The slope was 60-70 degrees at the top and gradually decreased to 30 degrees at the base. The sides and base of the slope were surrounded by boulder fields. The four had ascended the slope the previous day without ropes and without incident, except for a borrowed crampon that came loose on Daniel Savelson while ascending. This was resecured without further problems.

David was the first to rappel the initial pitch. The pitch ended at the steepest part of the slope. Prior to removing himself from rappel, David clipped into one ice ax with a daisy chain, thus using the ax to self-belay himself. Once off rappel he set up an anchor with two screws and webbing, and then clipped into the anchor, planning to carve the next bollard. By this time Daniel had rappelled down and was standing on the lip of a sun cup. He was about eight feet to the left and above the anchor, had taken his pack off and secured it to his ax. David removed his own pack and placed it with Daniel's. He was not hooked into the anchor, so David decided to chop out a flat area in the ice for him to stand on more safely. Before traversing over to below Daniel, David unclipped the daisy chain from his ax, presumably to make it fit easier to swing while chopping. He then unclipped from the anchor which was too far from Daniel. As he traversed over, David switched from front pointing to a modified French technique. At one point he stepped to the left with his right foot, but the crampon did not bite the slope and his foot slid down the ice, with him quickly following.

Instinctively, he instantly threw his ax into the slope in an attempt to self-arrest. However, he was sliding on his back and moving very rapidly down the slope, and the ax only scraped the surface. For a few seconds as he slid, he continued to try to push the ax (which was above and behind him) deeper, but to no avail. He began hitting the many sun cups in the slope, each acting as mini ramps, launching him in the air, and setting both him and his axes tumbling in every direction. He eventually lost consciousness and awoke lying on his back, head pointing downhill on the 30 degree slope, having fallen 400-500 feet and stopped 100 feet from the boulder field. He attempted to right himself but was unable to due to secondary pain from his broken femur. His friends spent the next 45 minutes setting up the rest of the rappels and safely lowering themselves down the slope.

He was moved to a flatter spot on the slope and covered with sleeping bags. Tony Ralf was sent for help. He ran for two and a half hours down the trail before he happened to be spotted by three Orange County police who were off the trail fishing. They had radios with them and called the closest ham repeater, apparently using an obscure frequency. A ham radio operator, who was working on his roof, heard his radio crackling and picked up the call and relayed it to Northern Inyo Sheriff Department. Mountain Rescue had just gone off duty within the last half hour but were still reachable. A helicopter was sent to the coordinates Tony gave using the map he was carrying.

Meanwhile Eric Savelson and Daniel were caring for David, who despite his injuries, was able to provide (according to Eric) helpful ideas for his own care. After checking C-spine as best they could, an ensolite pad was slid beneath him. He was given hot lemonade and some Gu. His fractured femur was placed in a traction splint using a ski pole and webbing. It was at that time that the fractures in his ankle were discovered. He was given some Tylenol with codeine for pain. The helicopter arrived three hours after the fall. With some difficulty the chopper managed to land on the slope. David was placed in a C-collar and then into a litter. An anchor was set up to belay the litter while it was moved down the slope and into the helicopter.

He was flown to Bishop Hospital where later in the evening (and into the next morning) he underwent surgery for his lower extremity fractures. He had lost half of his blood volume, most likely due to the femur fracture. Injury list included the displaced femur fracture, a distal fibula fracture, fracture of the talus in two planes, six broken ribs, broken nose, frontal sinus fracture (requiring surgery), concussion (would be dead without the helmet), dislocated A-C joint and partially torn deltoid in the right shoulder (probably from the attempted self-arrest), several facial lacerations, and various ligament sprains and partial tears. Total hospital time was two and a half weeks, including two days in the intensive care unit. (Source: David Lown, M.D.)

Analysis

The first mistake occurred the day prior to the accident. Since it was his first time climbing on ice, Daniel should have been roped up and belayed, especially near the top which was the steepest of the slope. Learning how to use technical axes and crampons should not be done in an environment where a mistake would be dangerous. An argument could be made for the roping up of the other three climbers; however, it was each one's decision not to (although the matter was not discussed prior to the climb and each just began climbing as they got to the slope, party separated—an example of poor team work). The other three had variable experience on ice and snow. All had at minimum led one pitch of technical ice and had experience with climbing in moderate alpine conditions. The climb the day before had been Daniel's first time on ice.

As for the accident, first Daniel should have clipped into the anchor prior to removing himself from rappel. If this was not feasible for whatever reason, a second anchor should have been created for him prior to coming off rappel. Given that neither of these occurred, David should have climbed next to Daniel and placed an anchor there. This would have assured Daniel's safety before any ledges were chopped out from beneath him.

Once David created the initial anchor, he should have made all attempts to remain clipped into it. He considered lengthening the webbing on the anchor so he would have more room to move; however, he only had two-foot runners and felt it would have been a hassle and clumsy to girth hitch them in a row to the anchor. In retrospect this is what should have been done.

While traversing on the ice he should have continued front pointing as the slope was pretty steep (60-70 degrees) and to French technique properly in plastic boots is very difficult. On the crucial step he did not place his boot perpendicular to the slope in proper French technique, thus his crampons did not bite the snow. Instead the edge/side of his boot contacted the slope and obviously provided no grip. Also this was his first outing using Black Diamond Switchblade crampons. In contrast to other crampons he had used, the outside edge of these crampons do not run flush with the edge of the boot, they are set in about a half inch from the edge. This also makes using French technique more difficult, as there is a high chance of doing exactly what he did.

He should have kept himself clipped into his ax with the daisy chain if he was not going to be connected to any anchors. If it was cumbersome to chop with the daisy attached, he could have had one ax free to chop with and the other planted firmly with a daisy attached to that one. Finally, for unknown reasons, he did not consistently and securely place his axes in the slope before each step. This goes against everything he believes in and teaches others. One must always maintain three secure points of contact when moving any limb. It is difficult to understand what caused him to stray from this golden rule at this point in time.

As far as the rescue itself, Eric, Daniel and Tony came through in a crisis situation in the way we all hope our friends would. Eric and Daniel provided excellent care (the traction splint was probably a life-saving maneuver) for a severely injured patient, although their only medical training was Wilderness First Aid. The only things that might have been done differently would be the early placement of an improvised C-spine collar and refraining from administering any narcotics to a potential head injury patient (a poor decision made by the patient). Both of these guidelines are based on the mechanism of injury and the high likelihood of both spinal injury (amazingly this did not occur) and head injury, even with a helmet. (This did occur and the facial injuries were a clue to this.) Lastly, elevating the legs and lowering the head is indicated for potential shock, although this might have placed the victim in unsafe position given terrain.

I would like to acknowledge the following people who played critical roles in the rescue and without whom a less than happy outcome might have occurred: Sgt. Kevin McKeown, Orange County Police; Jim Gilbreheh, private ham radio operator; Mike Brown, EMT and CHP helicopter pilot, Fresno, CA; Marshall Wharton, paramedic, CHP, Fresno; Deputy Randy Nixon, SAR Coordinator, North Inyo Sheriff Department;

Volunteers of Inyo County Sheriff Posse SAR Bob Wilson, Mark Lester, and Leonard Bayghenbaugh. (Source: David Lown, M.D.)

(Editor's Note: There were three other major accidents in this vicinity during the summer and fall. One was a solo climber doing a traverse of the Palisades who took a fatal fall out of Clyde Couloir. Another was an unroped climber on Mount Dana who fell 400-500 feet down a couloir to his death. The third involved a couple climbing in the Convict Lake Drainage of Red Slate Mountain in June. They fell several hundred feet to their death, probably because they were off route in poor weather and had no running protection. Gary Guenther, a member of the Mono County Mountain Rescue Team, provided as much information as he had on these. His interesting observation may have some bearing on the accidents. He stated that there was probably more snow left in the Sierras from the previous winter than from any winter in the past hundred years. He said that the fall of 1995 was also the driest fall on record. There were an additional four fatal hiking accidents and eight serious injuries resulting partially from the conditions.

Another indication of the severity and uniqueness of the conditions was that about 25 deer carcasses were found in the region and they were in positions that suggested they had reached a high velocity from uncontrolled slides.)

FALL ON SLICK ROCK, HASTE—APPOINTMENT AT THE BAR, "FAILURE TO RECOGNIZE THE..."
California, Yosemite Valley, El Capitan

Tim Sell and I had just finished climbing Mescalito (VI 5.9 A4) on El Capitan. It was Halloween evening. Although it was getting late, we thought we could make it down the rappels to the bottom of the East Ledges before it got dark.

We repacked our loads frantically, inadvertently burying our headlamps inside the haul bags. We had an appointment in a bar for 7 p.m.! We wanted to have more than a few beers with two climbers who had been a day ahead of us on Mescalito. As it turned out, it got dark more quickly than we expected. Rain seemed to be coming from the west, and we were having difficulty following the cairns in the light of a half-moon behind thin clouds.

At one point, we were just to the side of the actual trail and had to descend a not very steep, but very slick, slab. As Tim slid down the slab, he had his hand on his haul bag, which was sliding down the slab just beside him. I slid down more to the left, with my haul bag still on my back. I was immediately going faster than I had anticipated I would, and a big crack and ledge in the slab was coming up quickly. I tried to use my feet and hands for friction to slow down, but as soon as I did that—snap!! I yelled, "Compound fracture," even before I looked down at my twisted lower leg to see the huge bulging area about four inches above the ankle.

Tim did a great job splinting the leg with tubing from one of the portaledges. We had to stay put for the night. Since I was showing symptoms of shock he was afraid to leave me alone. Also, we decided it wasn't a good idea for him to try to find his way down the descent in the dark since he'd never been down the East Ledges before. At first light, Tim finished the descent and got help. I was shorthauled (helicopter) down to El Cap meadow about 2:00 p.m., and eventually ended up being helicoptered to Modesto to get a piece of hardware implanted in my leg.

My heartfelt gratitude to the Yosemite SAR Team for their excellent work, in a time when I imagine they are really strapped financially. Also, thanks to the Medi-Flight folks who got me to Modesto for emergency surgery in poor weather conditions.

Chalk up another one for *ANAM*; never thought it could be me! I'm still trying to figure out how it will read: "Failure to recognize the..." (Source: Tom McMillan, 39)

(Editor's Note: As we were going to press, we received four incident reports from Joshua Tree National Park, all of which are included in the data. Nina Burnell, NPS Ranger there, reported that one serious head injury was the result of mixing climbing with drinking, and that a high percentage of the rescues in JTNP are the result of inexperience and of not preparing for the descent.)

DARKNESS, STRANDED, RAPPEL ERROR—ROPE JAMMED
Colorado, Eldorado Canyon State Park, Red Garden Wall
On February 18, two climbers (one 24) became stranded when darkness fell and their rappel rope jammed on Red Garden Wall. They made a fire to keep warm, and were rescued the next day.

Analysis
One of the "Climb Smart" questions to ask: Is there enough light to finish the climb? (Source: Tim Metzger, Park Manager, Eldorado Canyon State Park)

FALLING ROCK, POOR POSITION
Colorado, Ouray, Dexter Creek Slabs
On February 26, the Ouray Mountain Rescue Team was called out to rescue Carroll Robinson (36), who had been struck on the head by a large rock. He and his partners, Dan Mays and Steve House, were rappelling at the time, and Robinson was tied into a belay station mid-way down. Robinson and Mays were lowered to the base of the route by House, who then ran to the nearest phone to summon the Ouray Mountain Rescue Team.

As mission commander and the first member on the scene, it appeared to me that there was not a lot that we were going to be able to do for the victim. It was late in the day and Robinson's vital signs were very poor. He was suffering from major head trauma as a result of the rock strike, and although he was wearing a helmet, it was of no use in this case as the impact was so great that it broke a carabiner he was attached to the belay with.

After the rest of the rescue team arrived at the base of the gully, which is approximately 750 feet above the road, it was determined that Robinson needed immediate helicopter transport if he was going to have a chance. We proceeded to do a short haul operation to bring him down to the waiting Airlife chopper. Unfortunately, he was not able to be revived at the hospital and the plugs to his machinery were removed several days later. Robinson's wife did choose to donate many of his usable organs so some good came out of this tragedy.

Analysis
Our area of mountains is considered one of the most dangerous in the United States. With the rapid change in weather here we have a high chance of avalanche and erosion goes on constantly. One minute it may be sunny and warm with a temperature of 70 and the next it may be windy, snowy and icy with a temperature of 20 or below depending on the wind chill. We have had accidents on our "fourteeners" in the middle of July when a storm blew in and some people were not prepared for the weather. We have people who come from sea level and climb the Sneffels Range and exhibit symptoms of high altitude

sickness as well as hypothermia. Our rescue time is also greatly hindered by the terrain.

In the Carroll Robinson incident, however, the accident occurred in an area in which we had just trained the week before. Arrival time and evacuation were relatively fast compared to other areas which take a minimum travel time of one hour.

The only mistake in this case was a disregard for the conditions. The party was on a south facing route on an extremely warm afternoon, with temperatures in the 45° to 50° range. (Sources: Bill Whitt, Lieutenant, and Nancy Chiltar, Secretary, Ouray Mountain Rescue)

CORNICE COLLAPSE, POOR POSITION
Colorado, San Juans, Engineer Mountain

On April 2, David Ganley (32), Fred Hutt (24), and Mike Seeberg (30) left Coal Bank Pass parking lot at 0700 on snowshoes to climb Engineer Mountain via the North Ridge. They left the snowshoes at the base of the ridge and proceeded to the summit wearing crampons. They were accompanied by a dog.

David Ganley was first to summit and was sitting on the cornice peeling an orange. Fred Hutt and Mike Seeberg were close behind. Fred also sat down, and Mike said something like, "That's not a good place to sit," as the cornice collapsed and the two men (and the dog) dropped off the north face. The cornice break appeared to be no larger than ten feet across.

Seeberg descended to the toe of avalanche debris, and determined that Ganley was dead and Hutt was in critical condition. (The dog was visible and mobile, but with a hip/leg injury.) Seeberg covered the injured victim with a parka and left to get help. Upon returning, Seeberg and flight nurse Leo Lloyd were lifted to a landing zone about a quarter mile from the scene, stabilized (oxygen administered) and packaged on Sked. They began dragging the victim out, and were assisted by Hogan and Bachman, who came in from the landing zone after being dropped by Air Care. The evacuation took about 45 minutes. The team was met by New Air Jet Ranger at the landing zone and the victim was loaded and lifted around 1715. The victim was delivered to Air Care at the staging area and transported to Mercy Hospital in Durango. New Air returned to drop two SJSAR personnel at the scene. Lloyd, Hogan and Bachman walked back to join them and the fatal victim was packaged. New Air returned and touched down under power, while the body was loaded and secured on the ship. New Air flew to the landing zone where the body was better secured and transported to the coroner at the staging area. The five personnel walked back to the landing zone with the dog and the party's gear and were lifted off, in turn, to the staging area.

Analysis

The actions of the witness, Mike Seeberg, contributed immeasurably to Fred Hutt's survival. Seeberg, seeing the location of the victims on the snowfield below the north face, rapidly retreated back down the ascent route to a couloir which exited on the snowfield several hundred yards to the south. Seeberg covered Ganley, and determined he had sustained obvious fatal head injuries. He performed effective first aid on Hutt's head injury, stabilized his position, wrapped him in a bivy bag along with spare clothing and raced to where their snowshoes were stashed at the bottom of the ridge. He then ran down the snow-covered terrain to where their car was parked and drove to a ski lodge at the base of the pass where he phoned the authorities.

The Air Care Helicopter from Durango was in the air on a training mission and was diverted to the wide highway in front of the lodge where it was met by the victim. Very little time was spent on the ground and Seeberg and Leo Lloyd, who is also a strong and experienced mountaineer, were lifted into the vicinity of the site and raced over snow to the victims. Hutt was then stabilized, given oxygen and packaged for the drag out to a suitable landing zone, where he was evacuated by a second helicopter to the waiting Air Care ship below, and taken to the Durango Hospital 27 miles to the south. Hutt's core temperature upon arrival at the Emergency Room was 86° F. (I believe he has made a full recovery.)

Were it not for Seeberg's decisive actions—reaching the scene, stabilizing the victim, racing to the parking lot and to a phone and then joining the initial rescue party to pinpoint the location and helping the flight nurse treat, package and drag out to the landing zone—Hutt would surely have died. Minutes made the difference.

Each victim suffered severe trauma, but little other impact injury after a fall of slightly over 1,000 feet, much of that nearly vertical. (The dog was virtually uninjured.) I theorize that the head injuries occurred early in the fall, but that enough snow was entrained in the descent to act as a cushioning envelope around the victims. The slope below the face upon which the avalanche ran out was probably about 45° which helped decelerate the fall velocity and minimized chances of further injury. Hutt remembers nothing beyond the cornice collapse and the first few feet of the fall. (Source: Don Bachman, Avalanche Forecaster—Colorado Avalanche Information Center, Silverton Office)

RAPPEL ERROR—ROPES UNEVEN
Colorado, Eldorado Canyon State Park, Hand Crack
On June 11, a climber (29) rappelled off the end of one-half of his rope and fell 30 feet. He indicated that his rappel rope was not doubled equally. (Source: Tim Metzger, Park Manager, Eldorado Canyon State Park)

FALL ON ROCK, FATIGUE, LATE START
Colorado, Rocky Mountain National Park, Hallett Peak
On July 15, at 1030, Robert Gould (53) and Kenneth Brenneman (55) left Bear Lake trailhead to do an ascent of the Northcutt-Carter Route on Hallett Peak. Upon arrival at the base of the North Face, they realized that their start was too late. So at noon, they began to climb the Hallett Chimney (III 5.6, A2) because they thought that this would be a fast and easy route. The chimney was wet and had patches of snow in parts, causing the climbers to move slowly and resort to aid at one point. At 1845, about 300 feet from the top of the route, Gould took a 35 foot fall on wet and muddy rock, becoming unconscious and unresponsive. Brenneman lowered Gould to the side of a snow field, tied off Gould at two points on his harness, placed all extra clothing on Gould, and rappelled ten 70-foot rope lengths to the base of the face. He then reported the accident to Rocky Mountain National Park SAR team. The rescue effort, which was initiated at 2230 upon Brenneman's report, took until 1245 on the following day. Gould was wearing a helmet, and this probably contributed to his survival of the head injuries. The intensive care unit at St. Anthony's Central Hospital in Denver, CO, said that Gould did not sustain any fractures from the accident but that he may take six months to a year to recover from the neurological injuries. He was able to recognize his wife and daughter within three days after the accident.

Analysis
According to the investigating ranger, Phil Akers, the following factors might have contributed to the accident. It was a poor route selection for a summer ascent. The route was wet with patches of snow. According to the Climbers Guide Book to Rocky Mountain National Park, the Hallett Chimney is "wet and dirty in the summer... usually ascended as an ice climb in the winter." According to Brenneman, Gould was becoming fatigued prior to the fall, and the two climbers started climbing late in the day. (Source: Jim Detterline, Long's Peak Supervisory Climbing Ranger, Rocky Mountain National Park)

FALL ON ROCK, WET ROCK, HASTE
Colorado, Rocky Mountain National Park, Hallett Peak
On July 29, Robert Logan (37) and Chris Weaver (25) were attempting the Culp-Bossier Route (III, 5.8) on Hallett Peak. While leading the second to last pitch around 1700, Logan encountered a wet section of rock of moderate difficulty. He attempted to hand-jam a wet off-hands crack but slipped and sustained a 20 foot lead fall. He received abrasions on his buttocks and experienced severe lower back pain due to three fractured lumbar vertebrae. Belayer Weaver and a nearby team of climbers (Ralph Burns and Andy Donson) were able to raise Logan to the top of the route, where his injuries were stabilized and rescue summoned.

Analysis
The efforts by Weaver, Burns, and Donson in completing a pitch and a half of raising are noteworthy and commendable. Consider stabilizing the injuries before moving the patient if possible. Logan was lucky in having stable fractures to his back. Had the fractures been unstable, he might have sustained additional injuries from the raising. (Source: Jim Detterline, Long's Peak Supervisory Climbing Ranger, Rocky Mountain National Park)

STRANDED, NO EQUIPMENT
Colorado, Rocky Mountain National Park, Hallett Peak
On August 17, 1995, Gabor Vereczi (25) and Zoltan Vereczi (23) were attempting the 400 foot high east face of the East Glacier Knob. The Hungarian climbers were not using technical equipment, and became stranded on separate ledges 150 feet from the top. Rocky Mountain National Park SAR team rappelled to them with equipment and belayed them to the top of the formation and down the descent route. They were both uninjured.

Analysis
An experienced solo, sans rope, rock climber may insure himself against being stranded by carrying a rope and some protection for emergencies. Some preview of the route by prior roped ascent might also be beneficial. However, the safest alternative is not to risk this style of ascent at all. (Source: Jim Detterline, Long's Peak Supervisory Climbing Ranger, Rocky Mountain National Park)

FALL ON ROCK, INADEQUATE PROTECTION, EXCEEDING ABILITIES
Colorado, Rocky Mountain National Park, Lumpy Ridge, The Pear Buttress
On September 3, 1995, David Charis-Mink (39) began climbing the standard 5.7 run-out start on The Pear Buttress (III, 5.8+) on the Book formation of Lumpy Ridge. Charis-

Mink said that he lost his grip about 20 feet up, causing him to fall to the ground. He fractured his lower left leg, requiring a litter evacuation by the Rocky Mountain National Park SAR team.

Analysis
This start of Pear Buttress is infamous for shedding itself of aspirant climbers. There is no protection for nearly 30 feet, yet this start is more popular than the off-width chimney, often wet, which is the alternative. You assume a sporting risk by deciding to lead this, and sometimes one loses. Charis-Mink was a 5.8 lead climber, and unprotected 5.7 may have been over-extending himself. (Source: Jim Detterline, Long's Peak Supervisory Climbing Ranger, Rocky Mountain National Park)

STRANDED, INEXPERIENCE, INADEQUATE EQUIPMENT, FEAR
Colorado, Eldorado Canyon State Park, Wind Tower
On September 10, two young men (20, 21) and a young woman (22) climbed up about 250 feet on the East Face of Wind Tower and became stranded when they could no longer continue up (small roof outcrop), and were unable to negotiate climbing down. The evacuation/rescue took about three and a half hours. Although they sustained no injuries, this was our most involved incident in the park last year. (Source: Tim Metzger, Park Manager, Eldorado Canyon State Park)

(Editor's Note: This is a very typical incident for Eldorado Canyon. The road side attractions are everywhere and accessible. One can see a range of activity. For example, during this same period, I saw a man who weighed about 200 pounds take five leader falls from the same place, 80 feet up from the road, where the climb began. His belayer, a 120 pound woman—unanchored—got slammed into the wall each time. I asked another woman who was watching what she thought. "I used to belay for him, but then I broke my arm...")

FALLING ROCK, INEXPERIENCE, OVERCROWDED ROUTE
Colorado, Rocky Mountain National Park, Hallett Peak
On September 4, Labor Day, Tom(40) and Ed (42) had planned to climb Culp-Bossier on Hallett Peak. We got a late start as we got to the base of the climb at 0815. Someone at the base said that there were eleven people on the route. Because of this we decided to climb the Love route (5.9) so that there wouldn't be anyone above us.

While we were getting ready to start, a couple of sport climber types came by. I call them sport climber types because they were going to climb this seven pitch face at 12,000 feet elevation in shorts, with no shirts and no rain gear that I could see. Also, they said that their primary climbing area was Table Mountain and Clear Creek Canyon in Golden, CO. They were going to climb Culp-Bossier also. I told them that there were eleven people on the route and they asked what we were doing. I told them. They said they would like to follow us up the same route. They wanted to see our guide book because they didn't have one.

Later they asked me of it would be OK if they passed us by taking an easier line to the right. I said it would be all right. They passed us and then got back on our route about 50 feet above us.

After they got above us, they were slow. They were kicking rocks off and dropped a couple pieces of gear. It was obvious that they didn't have very much experience at this sort of climbing. Tom and I were not climbing real fast, but we were quickly catching up with them.

At the top of the giant pedestal, which is about four pitches up including some simul-climbing, I heard a rock go by. It is hard to describe the exact sound. The only thing I can think of which sounds like that would be a bicycle pedal. I am sure that this is because it was spinning at a high rate of speed as a result of glancing off the face higher up. Only after it hit a ledge below us did we hear the people above us yell, "Rock."

A couple of minutes later I am looking up and see another rock falling toward us. I yell, "Rock," and press my body to the face. The rock hits the ledge that we are standing on to my right with a lot of force.

I look over at Tom. He says, "My arm is broken." At first I think he is kidding. He isn't. He is standing about 12 feet away, as we were moving the belay station to take advantage of a better line on the upper face. I belay him over to me and look at his arm. It is bleeding quite profusely. His whole side is soaked with blood and when he leans against the rock blood starts running down the rock.

I yell up at the two above us and say, "You just broke his arm." One of them was on the crux and looked down, but didn't say anything. This is the last we see of them. There are a couple of climbers near us on Culp-Bossier. They stop climbing and watch us. They look really competent and I am sure that they would try to help us if we ask. I don't ask because it would take a while for them to get to us, and it would put them at risk because they would have to traverse the blank upper face of Hallet.

After attaching Tom to the anchor, I do what I can for him in terms of first aid. I wrap his arm in a bandanna and tape it on to control the bleeding. We don't have anything with which to make a splint.

Now to get town ASAP, I set up a rappel. I will rappel down and hold the end of the rope to control Tom's rappel. I am heading for the large gully just to the east of the route. On the way down, we get the rope stuck and I have to solo back up to get it unstuck. After four full double rope rappels we get to a ledge with some trees. At this point I can make a splint after which Tom feels more comfortable.

Also, I see some hikers below. I call out and ask if they would get our packs and shoes from the base of the climb. They helped and did this, but, didn't stick around. This saved some time because it was going to be about a 200 foot vertical scramble back to the base of the climb over talus to get this stuff.

We do the last rappel. At the bottom we meet some other climbers. These guys have some triangular bandages with which we make a sling for Tom. One of these climbers says he is an EMT and wants to clean the wound. Tom and I don't feel like this is a good idea. Tom is an RN and I have first responder training. They also offer to help carry some of our gear out which we gladly accept. I get all of my stuff and Tom's stuff in my pack except one rope and Tom's climbing shoes which the other group carries. They are a great help and we both appreciate their help.

We walk out. Getting down to the lake is a little tricky but Tom gets down OK. Walking out, Tom is still dripping blood. His bleeding never really stopped until we got to the car and he stopped moving around. The total distance to the parking lot is just over three miles.

No one other than the people who helped us at the bottom of the climb were ever involved in getting us out. We didn't notify the Park Service about the accident.

Tom wants to go to the hospital where he works as a nurse. I know that the rock hit him at 1400. I don't remember when we got to the parking lot, but we got to the hospital at 2000. This was Labor Day and the traffic was bad going down the Canyon.

Tom's injury ended up being an open fracture of the radius in his right arm. The fracture was about two inches from the elbow and the bone was crushed. This injury required two surgeries and Tom was in the hospital from Monday night until Friday afternoon. Tom ends up having the upper two inches of the radius removed. This may result in some minor disability for him in the future.

Analysis
So what could we have done differently that would have prevented this?
- Get an earlier start?
- Not climb when people are above us? But we were the first people on the route until we were passed via easier ground.
- Not have let them pass us when they asked? Would this have prevented them from passing us?
- Maybe stop climbing for a while until the current climbing fad ends and all the sport climber types move on to the next trendy sport?

Sorry, but it's true. There are a lot of people out there today who don't know what they're doing. (Source: Ed, who wishes to leave it at that.)

LOSS OF CONTROL—VOLUNTARY GLISSADE, NO ICE AX LEASH SYSTEM
Colorado, Rocky Mountain National Park, Andrews Glacier
On September 16, Charles Bailey (37) slipped on Andrews Glacier while glissading. He lost his ice ax and was unable to stop himself. He slid hundreds of feet on icy surface before coming to rest into rocks at Andrews Tarn. Bailey received a serious head injury, and was flown out by Rocky Mountain National Park SAR team with St. Anthony's Flight for Life.

Analysis
No matter how experienced one is at glissading techniques (as was Bailey), it is always possible to lose control, especially when the snow is icy. Losing the ice ax can make it near impossible to self-arrest. One can roll over onto the belly with feet downhill and attempt to slow and stop by arching the back and pressing toes and elbows into the snow. This may be only partially effective or non-effective if the surface has iced up. The best prevention for this accident would've been the use of an ice ax leashing system. Wrist loops alone afford little protection if the slip was sudden and unexpected. (Source: Jim Detterline, Long's Peak Supervisory Climbing Ranger, Rocky Mountain National Park)

STRANDED, INADEQUATE EQUIPMENT, BAD ADVICE
Colorado, Rocky Mountain National Park, Long's Peak
On September 17, at 1140, two unidentified females (approximate ages 25) became stranded on the North Face of Long's Peak on the crack system adjacent to the south of the old Cables Route. They yelled for help, and Larry Solsvig (a technical climber without equipment) went to Chasm View to coach the stranded climbers. Solsvig sent a companion toward the Long's Peak Ranger Station to request assistance. Solsvig eventually caught the attention of a pair of technically equipped climbers who had just completed the Diamond and were descending the Cables Route. The Diamond climbers rappelled over to the two stranded climbers and lowered them down to Chasm View with rope.

Analysis

The two young women told Solsvig that they were both technical rock climbers from the Boulder area. They said that they had not brought equipment with them because a friend had recommended the Cables Route as an easy solo rock climb for them. Unfortunately, they ended up off route, unable to proceed due to ice on the face (and no ice equipment), and stranded on a small mossy ledge close to the upper edge of the Diamond.

There are several important points to ponder here. First, mountaineering routes (even the old "easy" ones) do generally require more route-finding ability than do most sport rock climbs. Second, the climbers failed to check conditions with park rangers or local guides, who would have informed them of the ice and snow hazard. Third, although solo climbing is not endorsed as a safe practice, there are methods to make it safer, such as roped solo belay techniques. At the very least, the wary and wise solo climbers will always want to have an option to back off (carry a rope and a few anchors) or won't climb anything that is too difficult for the individual to down climb. Last, Larry Solsvig should be commended for handling the incident in a safe, controlled manner, with attempting several options for assistance. (Source: Jim Detterline, Long's Peak Supervisory Climbing Ranger, Rocky Mountain National Park)

FALL ON ROCK, PLACED NO PROTECTION
Colorado, Eldorado Canyon State Park, T-2

On October 7, a climber (38) was beginning to lead the eighth pitch of T-2 when he fell 16 feet, hitting the wall with his foot, resulting in a fracture. He was experienced (18 years and 5.11 leader), and this probably helped in his self-rescue rappel to the bottom. (Source: Tim Metzger, Park Manager, Eldorado Canyon State Park)

RAPPEL ANCHOR ERROR—INADEQUATE PROTECTION, FALL ON ROCK, NO HARD HAT
Colorado, Rocky Mountain National Park, Lumpy Ridge

On December 2, Greg Levine (28) and a female companion decided to retreat from the first pitch of Hand Over Hand (I, 5.7) on Batman Rock at Lumpy Ridge. Levine, the leader, allowed his friend to rappel from a station of two stoppers he had set. When Levine's turn came to rappel, he removed one of the stoppers. The rappel anchor "failed," and Levine fell approximately 70 feet to the ground, wedging in a chimney. He was knocked unconscious (was not wearing a helmet), and sustained a flail chest, fractured left femur, and lacerated pancreas. His friend hiked out about one mile to get help from Rocky Mountain National Park SAR team. The complicated yet successful medical effort was led by Estes Park Ambulance EMT-P Jeff Ofsanko.

Analysis

There was a short additional pitch of 5.5 to top off on Batman Rock, but the hour was already late when the Levine party decided to back off the route. Levine's female partner was inexperienced, and Levine would have had an easier time training her at one of the area's numerous top-roping crags. Levine was attempting to treat a single stopper as an anchor system. It is not known as to how much experience Levine had placing "traditional" protection, but it is of note that all his stoppers were in new condition. (Source: Jim Detterline, Long's Peak Supervisory Climbing Ranger, Rocky Mountain National Park)

FALL ON ROCK—LOWERING ERROR
Idaho, City of Rocks National Reserve

On August 6, Emily Town (19) was leading an estimated 240 foot climb up Stripe Rock when she and her father Glen Town, who was lowering her down the rock, ran out of rope, according to Wallace Keck, Assistant Reserve Manager. She died instantly from severe head trauma, according to Cassia County Coroner Paul Young.

Analysis

Apparently Ms. Town had climbed past the base of the third stage and was descending back to it when the last of the rope slipped through her father's hands before he realized what was happening. Mr. Town probably did not realize how high his daughter had climbed and that he did not have enough rope to lower her.

Errors in belaying—which safeguards climbers with a rope—are a common cause of accidents, Keck said. The park has had four similar accidents in the last five to six years, and at least one other person has been killed. But hundreds of climbers complete their routes safely each year in the reserve. (Source: *The Times-News*, August 8, 1995)

(Editor's Note: An interesting comment from Ranger Brad Shilling regarding the cause of the above accident is that it was the seventh reported serious accident caused by a belayer letting the rope-end through the belay device. We received two other incident reports directly from the City of Rocks National Reserve this year just as we went to press. They are included in the statistics.)

FALL ON ROCK, IMPROPERLY PLACED BOLTS, EXCEEDING ABILITIES
Illinois, Drapers Bluff

On April 1, David Krupp (26) fell 30 feet from a 5.10 bolted route. He set out with three experienced climbers to ascend his first bolted route. He was a skilled beginner but had no experience using slings. The route was first attempted by one of his climbing partners who secured into the first bolt at ten feet, but fell while trying to sling the second bolt. Krupp took an offer to ascend, as would many new climbers who have not had the fear of a hard fall. He successfully clipped into the second bolt, approximately 18 feet, on his way toward the top. He then properly placed a sling in his third bolt (30 feet), but while pulling up his rope to clip into the sling, he fell. The second bolt slowed his descent, but allowed him to strike the ground sustaining a closed fracture of his right distal tibia and laceration on his head. He was properly cared for by his partner, Drew Coleman (29), who was a trained medic and a fellow medical student. Krupp began going into shock while waiting for the EMTs, who were not familiar with the area and subsequently had a slow response time. He was helicoptered to a hospital in the southern Illinois area for treatment and surgery. Five days later it was found that he had developed compartment syndrome, a very serious complication of fractures and falls that develops 12 to 24 hours after trauma that can lead to amputation or death. It is characterized by loss of sensation and motion and severe pain on passively moving affected areas—a complication all climbers should be aware of.

Analysis

Improperly placed bolts can allow the climber to hit the ground in instances such as this. When designing a route, it must be remembered that slack is drawn when clipping into the sling. Whenever a climber is to bolt a route, it is important to consider all possibilities in allowing a climber to hit the ground. Krupp would not have hit the ground if the third bolt was placed lower. Subsequent climbers place trust in their predecessor. In addition, the more experienced climbers should not have allowed him to climb until the danger of hitting the ground was clearly not a possibility. Furthermore, if Krupp had practiced using slings on a simpler route, he would not have had difficulties clipping the rope into his sling and might not have fallen. Mixing a poorly bolted route with an inexperienced climber is obviously a dangerous recipe. (Source: David Krupp, Dr. Dan Chavez)

FALL ON ICE, INADEQUATE PROTECTION
Maine, Acadia National Park, Dorr Mountain

About 1245 on January 8, Sam Woodward (50), an experienced climber from Surry, was almost at the top of a 70 foot ice route called "The Bulge" when he fell. He does not remember the cause of the fall.

Woodward had placed an ice screw about 30 feet above the start of the route. He then ran out the rope on easier angled ice with no additional protection. Park Ranger Jim Glover is quoted in the *Bangor Daily News* (January 9, 1995): "When the climber fell, his partner had no chance to hold him. The belayer did a pretty heads-up thing by jumping down ten feet to get tension on the rope, but he was unsuccessful."

Woodward landed on an ice covered trail at the base of the route. He remained conscious but he had trouble breathing and he had no sensation in his legs. It was later determined that internal bleeding put pressure on his lungs, and that his spinal cord was severed. He will not regain the use of his legs.

First aid was started by other climbers at the scene. Climbers, along with Acadia Park Rangers and members of the Mount Desert Island Search and Rescue Group, worked together on the rescue. After the search and rescue group arrived, Woodward was placed on a backboard, put into a sleeping bag and into a litter, and an IV with warm fluids was started. He was also given oxygen.

A helicopter from the Maine National Guard's 112th Medivac Unit arrived at the scene around 1510 and using a cable hoist lifted Woodward into the machine. He was flown to the Eastern Maine Medical Center in Bangor and taken immediately into the emergency room. According to Ranger Grover, "Had there been any additional delay, even half an hour, the outcome could have been tragically different. (*Bar Harbor Times*, January 12, 1995).

Analysis

Woodward was an experienced climber who was known for being safe. He and his partner were wearing helmets and had good equipment. Park Rangers George Leone and Jim Grover, and Woodward's climbing partner, Dwight Lanpher (40), say that Woodward was not doing anything reckless. The climbing was easy and the ice conditions were good with the temperature around 20°. After the fact, it is clear that Woodward did not place adequate protection. (Source: George Hurley)

FALLING ROCK, POOR POSITION
Maine, Mount Katahdin, Chimney Pond

On September 2, two parties—Michael Lanza (34) and Penny Beach (29) in one group, Bill Mistretta (?), Rick Baron (30) and Diane Mailloux (24) in the other—were climbing simultaneously. Lanza and Mistretta were at the top of the second lead looking for anchors for separate belay stances when Mistretta dislodged a rock described by Lanza as being two feet by three feet by several inches thick. The other three climbers were 150 feet below anchored together. Rick Baron tried to protect the other two climbers by shielding them with his body. He was struck by a cantaloupe sized rock above his left eye. His helmet was knocked off and he was thrown backwards eight or ten feet down the slope before his anchor stopped him. He did not regain consciousness and died probably within fifteen minutes.

Analysis
If possible, the belay site should be away from the line of fall of anything dislodged by the leader. This is especially important on higher and less stable cliffs like Cannon and Katahdin. In this case, two leaders were climbing above three other people who were close together at a belay anchor.

Irwin Caverly, the park director, said, "Rock slides are infrequent. This was one of those freak accidents." Michael Lanza said that when the group registered at the ranger station, a ranger suggested they change their planned route, and they did. Lanza added that it was not a particularly difficult climb. "One of the most frustrating things was that the route we took was well below our ability level." He and Rich Baron, who was the eighteenth person to die climbing in Baxter State Park, had been friends for twenty years and had done countless climbs together. (Source: George Hurley and Michael Lanza)

FALL ON ROCK
Maryland, Carderock
On May 16, I was half way up Jan's Face, a climb at the north end of the Carderock Climbing Area, when we heard someone calling, in a weak voice, "HELP, I think I have broken my leg." I called back, "We will be right there," and asked for a ride from my belayer. A woman climbing next to me and I started toward the sound of his voice.

I was about two steps behind her when we arrived at the patient. I said, "Hi, I am Art Dodds, an Emergency Medical Technician, and may I help you?" I was more surprised by the response from the woman than from Joe, the patient. She said, "Oh, thank God you are here!" It made me wonder what she was planning to do when she got there. I put on my gloves (I carry some in my wallet) and began my exam. I had no other gear. He had a probable broken fibula just above the right ankle and an abrasion to the knee. A quick neurological and pulses revealed nothing remarkable. I splinted his ankle with his jacket and the webbing he was using for a harness. The mechanism of injury was a fall while bouldering. He believed he did not hit his head or lose consciousness.

My problem was, should I call 911? The last time 911 was called, they responded with two ambulances, three fire trucks, and a Park Service helicopter for a similar injury. A news media helicopter also showed up. They also blocked the parking lot for about two hours while they hauled the litter up the cliff. The place where the incident happened is about 1,000 feet from the parking lot and down a 40 foot cliff.

Joe was eager to get to his car and believed he could hobble with some help. Great. I got on one side and another climber got the other. Once we got to level ground, I got him on my back and we walked to the parking lot. I had told Joe I would drive his car to the hospital ten minutes away if he would wait until I got my gear down. He elected to remove the splint and drive his car, standard transmission, to the hospital in Frederick, Maryland, about a 40-minute drive. I wished him well.

On the way to get my gear, I ran into three members of Maryland SAR. They said, "What have you been up to?" "Oh, I just finished a rescue." They thought I was joking until they noticed I was removing my rubber gloves to shake hands. (Source: Art Dodds, via Peter McCabe)

FALL ON ROCK—BLOCK OF ROCK CAME OFF, PROTECTION PULLED OUT, ROPE SHEATH CUT, NO HARD HAT
Maryland, Delaware Water Gap, Mount Tammany
On March 12, before noon, Ralph Chang (36), Bruce Pollock, and Randall Fairman began lead climbing on Mount Tammany. All three are experienced lead climbers. At 1245 Chang began to lead a climb called "Friends in High Places" (5.7). At 1300 Chang took a lead fall while trying to place a piece of protection. A climber from another group contacted National Park Service dispatch by portable phone at 1323 with information about the fall. Nine rangers performed a belayed carryout of approximately 750 feet. Chang was loaded into an ambulance at 1616.

The three had made a couple of climbs before Chang began the lead on "Friends in High Places." When Chang was approximately 40 feet from the base, he attempted to place a piece of protection. The block he was standing on gave way. He fell four to six feet onto his placed protection. This piece pulled from the rock. He fell to his next piece, which held, stopping the fall approximately 20 feet from the ground. His belayer (Pollock) lowered him to the ground.

When the Hasty Medical Ranger (Shreffler) arrived on scene at 1410, he found Chang at the base of the climb. Chang was in a sitting position, leaning against Pollock. Chang's chief complaint was pain in the left shoulder and cervical spine area. A C-collar was put on, and primary/secondary surveys done. Pollock maintained stabilization until Ranger Mennenoh arrived at 1445. Mennenoh and Shreffler prepared Chang for the carryout. The High Angle Rescue Team arrived at the scene at 1502. Chang was packaged in the Stokes litter and the belayed carryout began at 1520 along the base of the ridge and over large boulders. At 1609, Interstate 80 (west lane) was closed by NJ State Police. Chang was loaded into Portland Ambulance and enroute to the hospital at 1616. I-80 was immediately opened to traffic.

Chang suffered a dislocated left shoulder and a laceration on the scalp. He was released from the hospital later that evening.

Analysis
Each climber had eight to ten years of climbing experience and had climbed in the Delaware Water Gap area. Chang was using a Maxim 11mm static rope for the climb. The sheath on the rope was cut and pulled apart, with the core receiving little damage. Pollock and Fairman were wearing helmets; Chang was not. All had climbing shoes and newer climbing hardware. (Source: Richard Shreffler, Medical Ranger, Delaware Water Gap National Recreation Area)

(Editor's Note: The rock formation here has sharp edges exposed throughout, which is probably why the sheath on the rope got cut. The sheath on static rope is a little tougher than on dynamic rope.

At this same site, one other legitimate climber accident (as opposed to the many scrambler accidents) occurred to a youth (23) in a scouting group. He was being lowered, then asked to be allowed to down climb. He simply lost his footing, rotated on the rope—which held him—and collided with the rock, hitting his helmeted head so that he was momentarily unconscious.

This area is seeing an increase in climbing activity. Approaching the climbs from the bottom, one must go along the side of I-80 for about a quarter of a mile, walking on a cement barricade, as the wind from 18 wheelers pushes one toward the dense shrubs inland. Many climbers hike the trail and then rappel down from the top because of this.)

FALL ON ROCK, CLIMBING UNROPED, EXCEEDING ABILITIES
Massachusetts, Chapelbrook Reservation, Chapel Ledges
On August 10, Pam Chavis (25) fell 75 feet from Chapel Ledges, where she was attempting her first free-solo climb. She had reached for a handhold, shifted some of her weight to that hand, then slipped. She got away with one leg fractured and one broken ankle.

Analysis
Pam Chavis had little climbing experience, and this was only her second time at this particular site. The newspaper report quoted her as saying, "I'm not going to let that rock get the best of me." So it is presumed she'll climb there again—but hopefully not with "an attitude." (Sources: Jed Williamson and an article by Jacqueline Walsh in the August 20, 1995, *Springfield Republican*)

FALL ON ICE, INADEQUATE PROTECTION
Montana, Hyalite Canyon, Mummy II Route
On November 30, Stefan Mitrovich (26) and Rob (19) were climbing the Mummy's second pitch (150 feet, 3+/4-). Stefan led out the initial 100 foot, 70° slope with one placement (a titanium and Snarg screw equalized) just below the final steep curtain. Five to ten feet from the top, Stefan paused to reattach a crampon to his boot and figure out the next sequence of moves. After several minutes passed, his two ice tools popped out and the surrounding ice fractured. During his 30-45 foot fall, with stretch from his single 8.8 mm rope, the crampons, tools, and helmet fell off him. Fortunately, the fall caused no serious injury (a bruised elbow). Stefan was able to hike out by himself.

Analysis
The season had just begun and the ice was thin and extremely brittle near the top. A leader should have been questioned. My partner, Chris Lhost, and I had suggested setting a top rope, to test the quality of the climb. Three things should have been looked at: (1) After experiencing difficulties with his (SM) crampons and with the brittle nature of the climb, lowering off should have been an option. (2) Leading with one 8.8 mm rope added, through the stretch, to the length of the fall. This positioned him closer to rock outcrops. One 10.5 mm or two 8.8 mm ropes would have been better. (3) Leading out a great length little with or no protection could have led to a more distant, drastic fall.

In addition, there were several other ice climbing accidents that happened this year, from classic leader falls, protection failing due to "yo yo" style leading to attain a higher point, and to one person jumping off a climb (15 feet) because her rope did not touch the ground. The latter, after breaking an ankle and her tibia, did not know the possible effects of what a fall with a crampon on can do! (Source: John Gallagher)

FALL THROUGH SNOW—SPRUCE TRAP, OFF ROUTE, INADEQUATE EQUIPMENT—COMPASS
New Hampshire, Mount Washington, Raymond Cataract

On January 9, Kevin Rogers (33) and Mark Landry (30) of Portland, ME, made a successful ascent of Pinnacle Gully. Around 1300 they started their descent from the Alpine Garden, intending to use the Escape Hatch, a snow gully which climbers sometimes use as a way back to the floor of Huntington Ravine.

They failed to find the top of the Escape Hatch and instead continued down the trailless Raymond Cataract, the shallow gully between the major ravines. About 1430, Rogers fell into a spruce trap and twisted his left knee, tearing the meniscus (cartilage). He could not move his knee. Landry went for help, leaving Rogers about 1600. Landry reached the Harvard Cabin about 1700, but found no one there. There was no radio because it had been removed the previous day for repairs. He continued on to the AMC Pinkham Notch Camp and reported the accident.

While other rescuers were being assembled, Chris Joosen, the caretaker at the time at Hermit Lake, went up the Lion Head Trail and traversed across to a point high in Raymond Cataract. The temperature by this time (about 1945) was 0° F and the wind was about 35 mph. Joosen stayed in the middle of the Cataract as he descended until he found Rogers. Because Rogers and Landry were well equipped with warm clothes and food and water, Rogers was doing very well in spite of his long wait in cold conditions. He was sitting on the ropes and backpacks to insulate himself from the snow, and he was wearing extra clothing including a down parka. Joosen had with him a Norwegian hypothermia heater which he put around Rogers. After about half an hour, the two decided to try to traverse toward Lion Head. They were helped by Harvard hutkeeper, Mikko Immonen, who had joined them.

At Lion Head, these three were met by the main group of rescuers. They used ropes and a litter to transport Rogers to the Tuckerman Trail where Brad Ray, the USFS Snow Ranger, was waiting with a snowcat. They reached the AMC camp shortly after midnight.

Analysis

Rogers and Landry were well prepared and they completed their climb early enough in the day. Their mistakes were in route finding on the descent: first in not finding the top of the Escape Hatch, and secondly in continuing down Raymond Cataract. Once they realized that they had missed the Escape Hatch, they probably should have contoured around the top of Raymond Cataract to reach the Lion Head Trail. Going down the Cataract is usually a bad idea because of unconsolidated snow and the danger of falling into water under the snow.

Most ice climbers descend from routes in Huntington Ravine by following the Alpine Garden Trail south to join the Lion Head Trail where it runs east along the upper edge of Tuckerman Ravine. All of this route is marked by large cairns. If visibility is so poor that the cairns cannot be found, climbers can follow a compass reading southward—190°—from the top of Pinnacle or Central Gullies until they reach Tuckerman Ravine and the Lion Head Trail.

Ice climbers who want to descend more directly to the floor of Huntington Ravine should spend time during good weather exploring the terrain, and they should know the current snow conditions on the planned descent route. The Escape Hatch and the more technical descent which crosses the top of Odell's Gully and then goes down a ramp to South Gully can be dangerous because of very hard ice or because of avalanche conditions. When the weather turns severe while climbers are on an ice route, it is usually safest to rappel the route. (Source: George Hurley)

FALL ON SNOW/ICE COVERED ROCK, PROTECTION PULLED OUT
New Hampshire, Cannon Cliff, Omega

On March 13, Alan Cattabriga (35) started up Omega, an extremely difficult and dangerous mixed (ice, rock, verglas, and snow-covered rock) route on the east face of Cannon Cliff a few hundred feet south of the Whitney-Gilman Arête. Cattabriga placed protection near the ground and threaded a runner behind ice columns at 20 feet. Higher on the pitch he threaded another runner around a less solid ice column. His highest protection was a Spectre ice piton, a steel beak made for marginal conditions. He was above that and at a point about 40 to 45 feet above the ground, standing on his front points on a snow covered 80° rock slab, with no adequate holds for his hands, when his front points slipped. He fell and the top two protection points failed. He hit the ground before the better protection came into play.

Cattabriga suffered a broken tibia and fibula in his right leg and a broken scapula in his left shoulder. He also had extensive bruising to his left shoulder (with probable rotator cuff damage), left ribs, elbow, hip, and calf. The entire left side of his body turned black and blue a few days after the accident. He was wearing a helmet and received no head injuries.

Cattabriga's two climbing partners, Jim Shimberg and Ted Hammond, splinted Cattabriga's right leg and then tied his helmet over his right foot so that his foot would slide easily over the snow. Cattabriga then crawled feet first down the snow covered talus slope and then at times head first through the trees. The crawl to the road took four hours.

Analysis

Omega is "an extreme route which epitomized the desperate nature of modern ice climbs with its thinly-verglassed start [and] mixed climbing... . [It] rarely comes into shape" (p. 72, *An Ice Climber's Guide to Northern New England*, second edition, by Rick Wilcox). The three experienced climbers understood the risks of difficult climbing and marginal protection. After the accident, Cattabriga wanted a self-rescue—with help from his partners—because he believes in climbers being self-reliant if at all possible. (Sources: George Hurley, Alan Cattabriga, and Jim Shimberg)

FALL ON ROCK, INADEQUATE PROTECTION, EXCEEDING ABILITIES
New Hampshire, Cathedral Ledge, Intimidation

On May 21, Craig Johnson (26) was at the crux move on Intimidation (5.10) trying to place protection, but could not. So he "went for it." He made the crux and was about to put in protection when he slipped off "polished, moist rock." He fell 20 feet and hit a ledge just as the rope came tight. He broke both tibias and fibulas.

Analysis

Johnson "definitely recommends slinging two nuts to protect the crux." He also commented, "Make sure you are *leading* solid 5.10." (Source: Craig Johnson)

FALL ON ROCK, PROTECTION PULLED OUT
New Hampshire, Rumney Cliff, Holderness School Crack

On July 3, I was leading Holderness School Crack, which I have climbed at least 20 times and led (in fact I led it before the accident). I scrambled onto the ledge, started the climb and placed a directional nut near the bottom. I continued and placed a #1 Friend. I continued about ten feet past the Friend (a total of 25 to 30 feet above the ledge at the bottom). I believe my left foot slipped—though I only remember hitting the ground. The Friend pulled out. I landed on my back and hit my head. I was littered off the edge. My husband is a paramedic and directed the rescue as well as administered first aid. I went to Speare Hospital in Plymouth and was transferred to Lakes Region General Hospital. My injuries included cracked ribs (back), cracked left humerus, sprained ankle, severely broken right hand which was operated on and put back together with three screws. I had lots of typical Rumney abrasions all over my body and minor bleeds in my brain (detected on the CAT scan).

Analysis
I would have been dead if I didn't have my helmet on. It's hard to know exactly what happened. I was not climbing above my ability and I was not ill equipped. I may have been over-confident and so did not pay enough attention to the Friend placement. Having a cellular phone in the car made everything happen very fast. It was not a luxury but a serious part of rescue equipment. (Source: Susan Kennedy, 27)

STRANDED, EXCEEDING ABILITIES
New Hampshire, Cannon Cliff, Lakeview
On July 13, Eric Lougee, with two years of climbing experience, took his cousin, Donald Lougee (33), to Cannon Cliff for what Donald thought was to be an introductory climbing lesson. After a short lesson, the two men started up Lakeview. When Donald realized that they were headed for the top he objected, but his cousin insisted on continuing. Eric Lougee reached the top of the Old Man's head in the late afternoon. Donald was unable to climb the final crux flake, 50 feet below the top.

Eric left Donald on the slab below the crux and went down the climbers' trail to call for a rescue. Two rescuers reached the stranded climber at 2200. As one rescuer rappelled down to him, he saw climbing gear (protection and quick draws) in place in the exit corner, but no rope. The rope was in a pile at the beginner's feet where he was sitting on the slab. The leader must have dropped the rope, either intentionally or by accident.

Analysis
It is unfortunately fairly common for leaders to talk less experienced companions into climbing a route which is too difficult. In this case the beginner was not a willing companion. His first words to the rescuer were, "I told him I didn't want to do this. I told him!"

A more experienced leader could have helped his partner to the top in one of several ways. He could have hauled him using a Z pulley. He could have used his own weight as a counterbalance to help the second up the crux. He could have tied foot loops in his (the leader's) end of the rope, lowered those loops and anchored that end of the rope so that the second could climb the loops. He could have rappelled with the beginner to the brushy ledge below the Old Man's head and then bushwhacked north to meet the climber's trail. He could have taught his partner how to prussik before taking him onto a big cliff like Cannon. (Source: George Hurley)

STRANDED, OFF ROUTE, LATE START
New Hampshire, Cannon Cliff
On July 24, John (26) and Lisa Tedesco reached a spot close under the Old Man's chin on Cannon Cliff. They could not find the normal exit corner, the Wiessner finish, which

is the final pitch of Lakeview. They had bought a cellular phone for their trip to Cannon. (Their usual climbing area was the Shawangunks where the routes are short.) The time was late, they were confused about how to get off the cliff, and there had been rain showers, so around 1900 they telephoned 911.

Two rescuers rappelled down to the couple. The four people then rappelled another 40 feet to a brushy ledge which they followed north to meet the descent trail. They reached the Profile Lake parking lot at 0200 on the 25th.

Analysis
Lt. Eric Stohl of the New Hampshire Department of Fish and Game (in charge of all rescues in the State) was quoted in the Conway Daily Sun as saying that people should not expect a cellular phone to replace proper equipment, common sense, and an understanding of one's own limits while ... climbing. A cellular phone can be a great help, as it was in two serious rock climbing injuries this past season, but it should not take the place of self-sufficiency. (Source: George Hurley)

NOT ANCHORED AT BELAY—MISCOMMUNICATION, NO HARD HAT
New Hampshire, Cannon Cliff, Slip O' Fools
On October 1, Daniel Gelsomini (29) fell 35 to 40 feet from the top of the first pitch of Slip O' Fools at the north end of Cannon Cliff. He had reached the belay stance and called, "I'm off." Lori Gelsomini (29), Dan's wife and climbing partner, unlocked the carabiner which held the belay device. Before she removed the rope from the device, the rope started rushing through the belay plate. She looked up and saw Dan falling, with rocks falling with him. She was wearing a helmet, still anchored, and she was able to grab the moving rope and stop the falling, unconscious leader. She received second degree rope burns on both hands and arms.

Two other climbers, Randy Garcia and Will Higgins, from a nearby route, came to help Lori get Dan to the ground. Higgins then ran to his car phone to call for a rescue while the other two gave first aid.

Dan does not remember what caused him to fall. Lori Gelsomini thinks that Dan was struck by a rock falling from higher on the cliff (possibly from Lakeview which curves above the slab routes) before he was anchored. His skull was fractured in two places and his right eye immediately swelled shut. The force of the blow caused his brain to move forward suddenly, causing extreme swelling and bruising which resulted later in the loss of a small part of his frontal lobe.

Analysis
In her written account Lori Gelsomini says: "Always wear a helmet! It may not be the 'cool' thing to do but it can save your life. Clip into belay anchors immediately (before calling 'Off belay') even if you think you are safe."

Avoid climbing below other climbers. There are loose rocks on every cliff and Cannon is particularly unstable. (Source: George Hurley, Lori Gelsomini)

FALL ON ICE AND FROZEN MOSS, PLACED INADEQUATE PROTECTION
New Hampshire, Cannon Cliff, Black Dike
The ice on the Black Dike did not reach all the way to the top of the route on this Thanksgiving Day, November 23. Fred Abraham (35) was forced to climb frozen moss and thin

ice at the very top of the final pitch. When he was about three feet from the trees and easy ground, his tools pulled out. He fell and was caught by his next ice screw, a small Black Diamond. Because the talus bone in his ankle was broken, he set up an anchor and his partner, Brian Donelan (37), led on to the top. Brian helped Fred to the top and Fred then mainly crawled to their truck, taking about four-nd-a-half hours for the descent.

Analysis

Fred thinks that there may have been a bulge of ice under the handle of his ice tool and he may have levered the tool out because of that.

I have been in either the same place or in a similar place and have thrown a weight on the end of a long cord (17 feet of 7mm perlon) around a small tree at the top of the cliff. After tying the ends of the cord together, I had protection for the final few feet. The end of a haul line or one of two double ropes would work even better, since the leader could have a top rope belay. A few carabiners make a good weight for throwing; a third tool would be used to weight the rope since it might hook something solid even if it did not fall neatly around a tree.

Under some conditions rappelling the route rather than climbing a poorly formed final pitch would be wise. In this case, the two men discussed that option after the accident and decided against it, since the talus slope was not yet filled in with snow and because they were climbing with only one rope. (Source: George Hurley)

VARIOUS: FALLS ON ROCK, FALLING ROCK, PROTECTION PULLED OUT, INADEQUATE BELAYS, STRANDED, BEES
New York, Mohonk Preserve, Shawangunks

Of the 28 accidents reported from the Shawangunks in 1995, 17 were the result of falling, and in three cases, protection pulled out. The serious injuries included eleven fractures and one dislocation. There were two cases where the rappel rope did not reach the ground, and in one, the person rappelling unclipped and started to down climb when he found that his rappel rope did not reach the ground. He dislocated his shoulder when he fell. A man rappelling from Shockley's ceiling had to be rescued because he became stranded where the rope ended. Another fellow became stranded when he got stuck on Modern Times (5.8) and tried to prussik. His rope jammed, so he could not move.

There were six instances of falling rock, two of which were the result of climbers pulling a block of rock off. (A massive spontaneous rock fall was discovered in the Near traps days after it occurred.)

There was only one formal report of a bee attack, and that was on Classic (5.7). The climber got about 50 stings, but he did not fall or jump, and was all right. The rangers report that every year there are a number of accidents that go unreported because the injured person walks off or self-rescues. Yellow jacket and wasp attacks are common, but most go unreported.

The average age of the victims was 27, and the average difficulty of the climbing routes on which the incidents occurred was 5.6. This is about the same as in the previous year. (Source: Mohonk Preserve)

RAPPEL ERROR—CLIPPED TO ONE ROPE, FALL ON ROCK
Oregon, Smith Rock State Park

On February 4, John Elgin (24) fell 60 feet after failing to rig his rappel properly. All that is known is that another climber shouted to Elgin to recheck his rig as he prepared to rappel. Apparently he only clipped in to one of the double strands. (Source: Jeff Sheetz, Portland Mountain Rescue)

FALL ON ROCK WHILE SETTING UP RAPPEL
Oregon, Rocky Butte

On February 24, Allison O'Grady (21), a Pacific University junior, fell from the top of Rocky Butte as she and a companion were setting up a rappel so they could descend their climb of the butte. She suffered head injuries and was in critical condition. We do not know whether she was wearing a helmet. (Source: Jeff Sheetz, Portland Mountain Rescue)

FALL ON ICE
Oregon, Mount Hood, Leuthold Couloir

On May 28, approximately 0600: Three of us (Michele and Tim McCall, and Ken), climbers from Eugene Mountain Rescue, were climbing the Leuthold Couloir route. A party of six was ahead of us. The last rope team of two fell about half way up the route. The lead climber, George Garcia (46), fell; the second, Craig Sleight (38), attempted an arrest. George was already falling too fast and he pulled Craig off his arrest. George and Craig fell approximately 800 feet before their rope caught on an ice horn and stopped the fall (about 600 feet above a large crevasse).

We summoned the two other rope teams from the victims' party and quickly downclimbed to offer aid. We found the injured pair quite tangled in their rope and in much better condition than expected. Craig had several abrasions, a deep laceration in his thigh and a fractured arm. He was able to walk out with Ken to Illumination Saddle where the Timberline Lodge snowcat evacuated him. George was too seriously injured to walk. He was very disoriented and he had severe pain in his shoulders and ribs. The other members of his party reached us and we called for assistance on a cellular phone that they were carrying. We knew that it would be several hours before help would arrive and that it was too dangerous to stay in the couloir.

Tim, climbers from George's party, and I lowered George on belay with two attendants to a relatively safe place on the Reid Glacier. The lower took about four hours due to difficult terrain and George's condition. We secured George on the Glacier and monitored his vital signs. He appeared to be slipping into shock. Two medics from the American Medical RAT team arrived about five and a half hours after the fall. They treated George with fluids, oxygen, and pain medication which helped to stabilize George's deteriorating condition. About an hour later a helicopter and medics from the 304th Air Rescue of the Air Force Reserve arrived to evacuate George. Several climbers and the medics lowered George to the landing site and he was flown to the hospital.

Analysis

When climbing a route like Leuthold Couloir, a speedy ascent is essential. A party must ascend quickly to avoid ice and rock fall danger. When conditions feel comfortable, many people climb this route without protection. However, this accident shows that under these conditions the snow was too hard for one climber to hold another's fall. A running belay in this case probably would have held George's fall or at least slowed it enough for Craig to be able to hold his arrest.

With all of the talk today about the expense of climbing rescues, I want to comment that this rescue was handled mainly by the injured climbers' party and our party that just happened to be at the accident scene. Both parties were very well equipped for the evacuation and basic patient care. George's possible life-threatening injuries did require a helicopter evacuation, but in Oregon, the 304th uses this type of evacuation to qualify for training hours, so there is no cost to the public. (Source: Michele and Tim McCall, Eugene Mountain Rescue)

FALLING ROCK—DISLODGED, FALL ON SNOW, EXCEEDING ABILITIES, INADEQUATE EQUIPMENT/CLOTHING
Oregon, Mount Jefferson, Milk Creek

During the weekend of July 29-30, six teenage boys elected to climb Mount Jefferson via the Milk Creek route. Nearing the summit pinnacle, they drifted north, crossing the creek, and ascended steep snow without helmets and unroped. Not all had ice axes. Around 1430, a large boulder was dislodged by members of the party and rolled toward another member causing him to lose his footing. He took a tumbling, sliding fall of nearly 600 feet into Milk Creek couloir. During the fall, he sustained an open fracture of the left forearm, possible closed head injury, numerous lacerations, and although he did not know it, a fractured ankle. Dressed primarily in shorts and T-shirts, the six were not prepared to bivouac. Three remained with the injured teen while two descended to their camp at 6,400 feet to alert another member of their party before leaving for help. By 2000, the injured boy, who had been unconscious following the fall, was more lucid, and his friends began assisting him toward their camp, 3,000 feet below. They arrived in camp around 0230.

CMRU Mission Coordinator, Bill Ellison, received a call at 1915, and at Bill's direction, Benton County paged CMRU at 1930. The truck was underway before 2100 and arrived at the Pamelia Lake Trailhead about 2300. Shortly after midnight, CMRU, ESAR, and Posse teams were in the field heading toward the jump off point on the Pacific Crest Trail. CMRU and ESAR teams carried gear up the mountain and located the camp at 0543. While the medical team assessed the patient and checked out others in the climbing group who sustained minor injuries, the remaining teams arrived with evacuation gear. Medical information was passed to the 304th ARRS and they launched two helicopters plus a C130.

The helicopters arrived on scene at 0902 and inserted two PJs with a backboard and litter. The patient was transferred from CMRU's litter to 304th's and packaged for helicopter evac. The helicopter returned and maintained a seven-foot hover while the litter and patient were placed aboard. The PJs scrambled aboard and the evacuation was complete at 0949. Field teams packed up gear and departed the scene at 1023, arrived at the PCT at 1136, and returned to base camp by 1400.

This was a very smooth mission with excellent cooperation among the various units. PMR had sent three personnel who patiently waited in Base Camp.

Analysis
This party had little or no mountaineering experience. It is interesting to note that this accident occurred at 1430 in the afternoon, while they were *ascending* around 9,500 feet. It is strongly advised that climbers get a very early (0100 to 0300) start when climbing such routes. During the summer, the snow and ice covered volcanoes of the Cascades experience rapid softening of the snow, and often copious rockfall once the sun rises.

Not all of the members of this party had ice axes or crampons. They chose to leave most of their shell and insulating clothing at camp and climb in T-shirts and shorts. Helmets were not worn. Obviously, had they had this clothing, it may have prevented an epic descent with a disoriented climber. This descent included many falls, some into the creek, and nearly over a waterfall. (Source: Jeremy N. Adolf, Corvalis Mountain Rescue Unit)

FALL ON ROCK, CLIMBING UNROPED
Oregon, Rocky Butte
On August 19, Larry Anglin (31) was free climbing an 80 foot practice cliff, fell, and sustained critical head injuries. Subject was not wearing a helmet, but it is unlikely that a helmet would have made any difference. It is not known why Mr. Anglin climbed a moderate 5th class practice route without a belay, despite his use of a seat harness and trailing climbing rope. Belay-less climbing is not generally recommended, especially when long falls can occur.

PMR was not requested to respond. Above information obtained from newspaper article and discussion with Gene Gray, medical examiner. (Source: Jeff Sheetz, Portland Mountain Rescue)

OVERDUE—MISSING, PROBABLY FALL ON ROCK/SNOW, CLIMBING ALONE
Oregon, Mount Hood, Cathedral Ridge
Ken Budlong (45), an experienced Portland climber, was reported overdue from a solo climb of Cathedral Ridge on Monday, September 26. On Sunday night he phoned home with his cellular at high camp and conveyed his plan to ascend the route if the weather was favorable on Monday morning. Ground searchers located his unoccupied tent on the ridge at 7,000 foot elevation. Searchers battled stormy, wet weather for the next four days. On Sunday the weather improved and supported an extensive ground search and three military helicopters. No signs of Budlong were found. The previous storm had dumped at least three feet of avalanche-prone snow on the upper reaches of the mountain. Budlong had summitted Mount Hood over twenty times. It is probable that he fell while high on the route, injuring himself when he landed in a crevasse or moat.

Analysis
The Cathedral Ridge route, although remote, is not considered difficult or an unreasonable pursuit for experienced climbers. Budlong was well equipped, but was afflicted with a "trick" knee. Solo climbing almost always increases the risk of any climb. (Source: Jeff Sheetz, Portland Mountain Rescue)

FALL ON ROCK, INADEQUATE PROTECTION
Utah, Wasatch Mountains, Parleys Canyon
On March 19, Guy Riley (25) fell while climbing on a popular rock buttress at the mouth of Parleys Canyon. Details were somewhat sketchy, but Mr. Riley's protection apparently pulled while on lead, causing him to fall approximately 15 feet to the ground. The Sheriff's SAR team evacuated him and he was transported to a local hospital by ambulance.

Analysis
Although we don't know the experience level of this particular climber, this area is very popular with young climbers fresh out of the climbing gyms. (Source: G. Banks, Salt Lake County Sheriff SAR)

FALL ON ROCK, INADEQUATE EQUIPMENT
Utah, Wasatch Mountains, Big Cottonwood Canyon
On April 26, Brandon Keller (22) fell while leading "Skyscraper," a one pitch climb, in Big Cottonwood Canyon. Keller suffered injuries to his head, neck, and back as a result of the fall. Witnesses indicated that Keller was leading, and was up approximately 25 feet when he tried to place some protection, which he missed, and fell to the base of the climb. The victim was lowered to the highway by litter, and transported to the hospital by Life Flight Helicopter.

Analysis
No other protection was found, and it appears that the subject climber was trying to place his first piece of protection (25 feet) when he fell. Upon interviewing the witness, it appears that no one was even on active belay. (Source: G. Banks, Salt Lake County Sheriff SAR)

FALL ON ROCK, RAPPEL ERROR—ANCHOR KNOT FAILED
Utah, Wasatch Mountains, Big Cottonwood Canyon
On June 17, Harmer Kirt fell while rappelling at Storm Mountain in Big Cottonwood Canyon. Kirt fell 15 to 20 feet and injured his ankle and wrist. Mr. Kirt was removed by the Sheriff's SAR team and transported by ambulance to the hospital.

Analysis
Investigation revealed that the subject's anchor knot had failed. (Source: G. Banks, Salt Lake County Sheriff SAR)

FALL ON ROCK, PROTECTION PULLED OUT
Utah, Wasatch Mountains, Big Cottonwood Canyon
On June 23, Bryce Perkins fell while leading a climbing route in Big Cottonwood Canyon. Mr. Perkins' fall of approximately 60 feet, resulted in injuries to his head, back and one ankle. His belayer indicated that Perkins slipped while making a move, and as he fell, all of his protection pulled, slowing his descent, but landing him in a precarious position on a ledge. The Sheriff's SAR team responded to the scene, approximately 1500 feet above the canyon highway, stabilized the victim, and lowered him to the highway, where he was transported to the hospital.

Analysis
This particular area of the canyon is not often frequented by the climbing community, as a long, steep approach through loose scree fields is required to reach this buttress. We are seeing a higher incidence of accidents involving protection placement problems. (Source: G. Banks, Salt Lake County Sheriff SAR)

OVERDUE CLIMBERS—OFF ROUTE, INADEQUATE EQUIPMENT, PARTY SEPARATED, INEXPERIENCE, EXHAUSTION, DEHYDRATION
Utah, Wasatch Mountains, Lisa Falls Couloir
On June 26, the Salt Lake County Sheriff's SAR team was notified that two members, from an original group of five mountaineers, were overdue and presumed lost or in-

jured. The trip had begun the previous day, with a group of five climbers, which started an ascent up Tanners Gulch to the Big Cottonwood Ridge, west to Twin Peak, and then a planned descent down the Lisa Falls couloir, back to the canyon highway. This climb is known as "Cathedral Traverse," and in the spring or early summer, ice axes and ropes are strongly recommended.

Two of the members were moving somewhat slower than the rest of the group, and a decision was made to split up, with the faster three moving ahead, and ultimately, completing the route in the dark, on June 25. One rope and one ice ax were left with the slower two members. Just before dark one of the climbers in the lead group thought that he saw two people rappelling down a steep snow field above and behind them.

The following day, after the SAR team arrived, a lengthy interview was conducted with the complainants and it was learned that the two missing parties consisted of Bill Foster, most experienced and the team leader, and Susan Ryan, least experienced and a first timer for this kind of trip. Since a possible sighting had been made the night before, a search team was started up the Lisa Falls couloir, and the Sheriff's helicopter was dispatched to conduct an air search of the entire route.

After several hours of searching the Sheriff's helicopter spotted the two missing climbers, still high and near the top of the Lisa Falls couloir. The ground search team that had been dispatched earlier reached the two parties about an hour later. Both individuals were totally exhausted and dehydrated, but otherwise okay. Nearly six hours were required to assist the exhausted climbers back to the trail head.

Analysis
An interview was conducted with the two individuals and it was learned that shortly after separating from the main group, Susan became very intimidated by the exposure and was very tired as well. They spent a cold night just below the summit of the East Twin Peak (11,300 feet). They began moving down the next morning, but found the snow very firm and difficult with just one ice ax. Their progress was slow, and as they descended, they said that they saw the rescue helicopter several times, but were not successful in signaling it. (They were not the same party seen rappelling the night before.) The rescue team noted that both parties moved very slowly and had a difficult time with the Class 4 terrain. At times, simple commands had to be repeated, apparently due to their exhaustion and dehydration. (Source: G. Banks, Salt Lake County Sheriff SAR)

FALL ON ROCK, CLIMBING UNROPED, INEXPERIENCE
Utah, Wasatch Mountains, Mount Olympus
On June 29, Michael Fox and two companions were hiking in the North Fork, below Mount Olympus. Along the way, they encountered a rock buttress that Michael decided to free climb. After attaining about 40 feet in height, he lost his footing and fell to the bottom of the buttress. His companions determined that Michael was unconscious and appeared to be seriously injured. One of his companions returned to the trail head and notified the Sheriff's office.

The Sheriff's SAR team and paramedics from the Fire Department responded to the scene and found the victim in extremely critical condition. The victim had obvious head injuries and suspected internal injuries. He was quickly carried to the trail head (1/2 mile) and transported by air ambulance to the hospital. The victim died enroute to the hospital.

Analysis
The scene was investigated by the SAR team. The buttress consisted of mostly poor and crumbling holds and approached 5.8 in difficulty. The victim had no previous experience and no climbing equipment to secure himself to the buttress. (Source: G. Banks, Salt Lake County Sheriff SAR)

FALL ON ROCK, FAILURE TO FOLLOW INSTRUCTIONS
Utah, Wasatch Mountains, Big Cottonwood Canyon
On July 5, Karen Wilson, a student in an organized climbing course, took an unroped fall of approximately eight feet. Miss Wilson had completed her turn climbing and rappelling, and had removed her climbing harness and climbing helmet, so that she could slip off and go to the bathroom. Upon returning, she climbed up on the rock buttress to observe the other students and fell off, hitting her head.

The Sheriff's SAR team responded and carried her to the trail head where she was transported to the hospital by ambulance.

Analysis
The climbing school instructors were interviewed, and they indicated that they had reminded all of the students present, several times, to use care and not take off their protective equipment. The ratio of instructors to students looked adequate, and no negligence was noted. (Source: G. Banks, Salt Lake County Sheriff SAR)

LOSS OF CONTROL—VOLUNTARY GLISSADE
Washington, Guy Peak
On January 7, John Hughes (46) climbed Guy Peak with four other experienced friends. He was just starting to descend when he slipped from his glissade and could not self-arrest. He yelled, "Out of the way," and fell 1,000 feet down the standard route, over at least two cliff bands, coming to rest on scree. Witnesses spent 20 minutes attending to him, but he did not survive. (Source: From an MRA report by Debby Riehl)

CEREBRAL EDEMA
Washington, Mount Rainier
At 1030 on June 16, the climbing team of volunteers Dave Turner, Jim Funsten, and I met Todd Auker (37) and his rope mates Dave Walters and Scott Weir on the summit of Mount Rainier, in mildly lousy weather. Auker made the comment, "I think my brain stem is pushing through my foramen magnum," which I understood to be an amusing way of saying that he felt altitude sick, and had early symptoms of cerebral edema.

My party waited for a half hour to descend in order to be the last climbers down the Disappointment Cleaver Route and to search for overdue Liberty Ridge climbers. At 1120 we found Auker at 13,800 feet, descending very slowly. We stayed behind to be able to assist if needed. At 1130 Auker stopped to vomit. He said he had vomited on the summit earlier, and complained of a painful headache and intermittent ataxia and disorientation. Both Auker, a doctor, and I suspected altitude sickness and possible cerebral edema, for which descent is required.

I suggested that Auker would be able to descend more efficiently if he traded his ax for a pair of ski poles to improve his balance. He said his rope team was technically weak, so that he wanted to keep his ax for self-arrest unless I tied into his rope. Our rope teams joined. I attempted to report to the park communications center, but my radio battery failed. We descended slowly to the top of The Cleaver, arriving at 1340.

Auker was cold so I put my down parka on him. I gave him water and orange drink. I switched radio batteries and notified communications center of our progress. Our climbing party rearranged itself on our ropes so that I was immediately behind Auker. (I showed him how I had tied him in. Later, when he felt better, he said he couldn't recognize the knots I had used, even though they are familiar to him.) For the descent of The Cleaver, I held the rope a few feet from Auker's harness and had him slide on his back while I plunge-stepped to control his speed. Turner and Funsten were alert to help me arrest a slip. Auker walked leftward traverses to stay on the cleaver, and rested by glissading the fall-line portions.

He felt much improved at Ingraham Flats. We arrived at Camp Muir about 1615. Auker rested while Walters and Weir packed their camp. Turner, Funsten and I packed our gear, leaving Auker under Walters' eye. Walters is a doctor with EMT/ski patrol experience, familiar with high-altitude medical problems. RMI guides filled three water bottles for me to give the Auker party to save them the time of melting snow.

When we were packed I returned to check on Auker and accompany him on his descent. He felt weak enough that we decided to take him out in a toboggan. I gave him supplemental oxygen at four liters per minute through a nasal canula. Funsten's friend agreed to assist in our descent to Paradise. Ranger Jennifer Erxleben helped prepare the toboggan and package Auker in it. RMI guides offered to monitor the park radio in case we encountered problems in the evacuation. My second radio battery failed as I updated the communications center of our plans. We left Muir at 1830 and arrived at Pebble Creek at 1930. Auker felt sufficiently improved that he preferred to walk the rest of the way. We arrived at Paradise at 2050. I encouraged Auker to see a doctor and left him in the care of Walters and Weir. (Source: John Gillett, NPS Ranger, Mount Rainier National Park)

(Editor's Note: There was another case of cerebral edema in WA, this one on Mount Adams at the 9,000 foot level. The victim became very combative. His partner was able to get a 911 call through on a cellular phone. A helicopter evacuation in the early morning hours probably saved the victim's life. He was back at work within a week, but does not plan to go above 8,000 feet in the future.)

LOSS OF CONTROL—VOLUNTARY GLISSADE, NO HARD HAT
Washington, Mount Stuart

On the morning of June 25, Gordon Rieker (31) and Chuck Buzzard (40) left their base camp at 0315 and headed up Ulrich's Couloir, a narrow gully leading to the summit of Mount Stuart.

The two Yakima County employees were not novice climbers. Rieker had been climbing since the early 1980s, Buzzard since 1978. Nor were they strangers to Mount Stuart. This was Buzzard's fourth climb, and Rieker had at least five previous climbs on the mountain. They also had made numerous climbs together.

They reached the summit about 0645. Instead of returning the same way, they headed east to the Cascadian Couloir, which is generally considered one of the least difficult routes on the mountain. Not far from the summit, they reached a long, steep snow slope where they began glissading, a standard mountaineering practice of sliding while using an ice ax to control speed. Buzzard went first.

"I was out ahead, nearly to the boulders. I looked up and he was doing a regular sitting glissade," Buzzard said.

But something caused Rieker to lose his ice ax. Unable to control his speed, he began an uncontrolled slide into the rocks.

"It happened so fast it's hard to picture," Buzzard said.

The impact broke Rieker's collarbone and several ribs, and caused severe head injuries. He appeared conscious but was unable to respond, Buzzard said. About ten minutes later, two other climbers discovered the Yakima men. They stayed with Rieker, and Buzzard began a long walk out for help.

Off the mountain, he still had to climb another smaller ridge before reaching the car. He then drove to a horse camp. But the camp's radio had been vandalized and wasn't working, Buzzard said. A woman at the camp had a cellular phone, but that required additional driving to reach a point where the phone's signal could be picked up.

Typically, U.S. Army MAST helicopters from Yakima Training Center are dispatched for back-country rescues. But this accident occurred at an elevation of 8,400 feet. That's considered too high for the standard single-engine MAST helicopter, which generally isn't used above 7,000 feet. Instead, a more powerful helicopter had to be dispatched from Fairchild Air Force Base in Spokane.

Initially, doctors were optimistic about Rieker's condition. But he died at Yakima Valley Memorial Hospital seven days after the accident. (Source: *Yakima Herald*, from an article by Craig Torianello, July 23, 1995.)

RAPPEL ANCHOR FAILURE—ROCK BROKE LOOSE, FALL ON ROCK
Washington, Mount Stuart

On July 10, Kris Stout (30) and his climbing partner had waited out a storm on Mount Stuart before beginning their descent. Stout was preparing to descend by rope when he tied a line around a rock the size of a car.

As Stout leaned back to begin rappelling, the rock broke loose. It rolled over him and fell 150 feet. One climber said the rock should have been there for another 100,000 years.

Stout's partner was left alone on the ledge, where he waited five hours until he was rescued by other climbers. (Source: *Yakima Herald*, from an article by Craig Torianello, July 23, 1995)

FALL ON SNOW—UNABLE TO SELF-ARREST, CLIMBING ALONE, HASTE—RESULTING IN WEARING ROCK SHOES ON SNOW
Washington, Mount Stuart

After summiting Mount Baker in the early morning of July 9, I drove about 3/4 of the way to Seattle and got a hotel room to dry out gear and repack for a solo attempt of Mount Stuart. On the 10th, I drove from the hotel to the parking area south of the mountain and hiked the four hour approach which brought me to the grassy slopes beneath the West Ridge (4,500 feet). The route planned on was the "West Ridge Route" as described in the Cascade Alpine Guide, Volume 1 by Fred Becky. I made camp and went to bed early. The weather was clear and the temperature dropped a little below freezing that night.

I began climbing at 0600 on the 11th, a cool morning with perfectly clear skies. I was climbing continuously up the snow couloirs and rock mainly 5.4 and below, but with problems reaching the 5.6 level.

There was a lot of snow still left in the couloirs. In the morning the snow was well consolidated from the night's freeze. The transition from snow to rock occurred several times on my way to 9,000 feet. This required me to change from double plastics to rock shoes several times. I reached a point near 9,000 feet on the ridge above the couloirs where the ridge stays mainly rock to the summit. While traversing just below the ridge crest east toward the summit, I encountered a finger of snow about 35 feet wide at a 40 to 45 degree angle. A committing problem blocked the way above the snow and a scary down climb below. I decided to traverse the snow to the rock on the other side.

Near the summit and eager to finish the route, I decided to cross the snow while still wearing my rock shoes. About half of the way across, the steps I had chopped/kicked gave way and I began sliding down the face. The snow had developed a top layer about six inches deep that was of very poor quality with still frozen snow beneath. I had my ax blade buried into the snow the entire time I was sliding down the face of the finger. The ax provided little if any reduction in my speed and the rock shoes were worthless. Just before hitting the rocks 40 feet below where I started falling, I let the ax go so it would not impale me during the impending tumble.

I hit the uneven rocks with both feet, badly bruising the heel bone in my right foot and spraining my left knee. I rolled across the left side of my body in a kind of half cartwheel and came to rest in a sitting position looking down the mountain. Luckily I could still walk and I actually finished the route at 1200 so I could be sure of finding the Southeast Route descent. I glissaded as much as possible on the descent and made it back to the tent at 1830.

After sleeping some I packed up the next morning and hiked the 3 1/2 hours out in six hours and a lot of pain. I asked two different sets of hikers for assistance while on the trail out, but since I could actually walk on my own, I was reluctantly denied any help. After reaching the car I went to the emergency room to have my foot X-rayed (no broken bones) and my knee drained. (Source: Gehrig Austin, Jr.)

FALL ON SNOW—CRAMPON CAUGHT IN CLOTHING, UNABLE TO SELF-ARREST
Washington, Mount Stuart

On July 16, Teresa Soucie (41)—a member of the King County Search and Rescue Team—was beginning her descent of the Cascadian Couloir on Mount Stuart when she tripped after apparently catching her crampon on a piece of clothing. She slid 300 feet into a rock pile, resulting in a broken rib and bruised pelvis.

Analysis

"It's a very attractive climb. It's a very beautiful mountain and it's attractive from a distance... and the approach from the south side is relatively short," said Ellensburg resident Fred Stanley (51), who along with famed Seattle climber Jim Wickwire pioneered the first ascent of a wall known as the Great Gendarme on Mount Stuart in 1964.

The 1979 publication of "Fifty Classic Climbs," which includes a Mount Stuart route, helped further popularize the mountain, he said. Stanley said most accidents occur on the south side for several reasons. As the easier way up, the south side attracts less experienced climbers. It is also used as a return route by experienced climbers who make more difficult ascents elsewhere on the mountain. In both cases, climbers can be tired. The combination of steep snow slopes and tired climbers can mean trouble, he said.

The south slope isn't steep enough to generally require ropes, although at 35 to 40 degrees, it's plenty steep enough to trigger uncontrolled slides. Some climbers have called it deceptive.

Fred Dunham, a 55-year-old Ellensburg resident who has lost track of how many times he's climbed Mount Stuart since his first ascent 35 years ago, isn't comfortable with that description.

"I would shy away from calling it deceptive," he said. "I say it's the way it is in the mountains." (Source: *Yakima Herald*, from an article by Craig Torianello, July 23, 1995)

LOSS OF CONTROL—VOLUNTARY GLISSADE
Washington, Mount Baker
On July 18, Robert Porter (48) was descending the Coleman Glacier on Mount Baker when he lost control of his glissade and tumbled into a crevasse, landing on a kind of saddle that kept him from going in deeper.

He managed to throw a rope out to his partner, who pulled him out. He was helicoptered out from there, and was in satisfactory condition in the hospital by the next day.

He was the fifth person in two years to have this kind of accident here. (Source: *The Bellingham Herald*, from an article by Mark Porter, July 19, 1995)

FALLS ON SNOW AND ICE, INADEQUATE EQUIPMENT—CRAMPONS WRONG SIZE AND BROKEN, MODERATE EXPERIENCE
Washington, Mount Rainier
On Saturday, August 12, John Craver (40) of Santa Cruz, CA, was descending with companions from the summit of Mount Rainier to Camp Schurman on the upper Emmons Glacier. While attempting to cross the bergschrund at 13,400 feet, he broke his ankle. Two other climbers returned over the top of Rainier and reported the accident to the climbing ranger at Camp Muir around 1700 after descending the Disappointment Cleaver route.

SMR member Luke Reinsma had standby duty at Camp Schurman on the weekend of August 12-13. Luke checked in at the White River Ranger Station and left the White River Campground at 1000 on August 12. He reached Camp Schurman at 1600 feeling tired and not ready to climb the next day. The seasonal Climbing Ranger Sean Ryan (23) was not there when he arrived, so Reinsma pitched his two-man tent and began preparing food and getting ready to get some sleep. Sean and another Seasonal Ranger, Phil Otis (22), arrived about 1700 via the top of Steamboat Prow, and immediately upon arriving and meeting Luke, asked him if he would like to climb with them the next morning. Luke declined, saying that he thought he needed to sleep. Sean began melting water in preparation for cooking a meal. About 1730, word came from White River on the radio that an accident had occurred high on the mountain, about 13,400 feet. The weather was overcast and cold, with winds blowing up to 40 mph, and it was reported that the party of three was without bivy equipment or fuel. Furthermore, it became clear that rangers on the Muir side were not able to respond immediately, and that the first response would probably have to come from the group at Camp Schurman. Sean, Phil, and Luke quickly ate and prepared to climb to assist the injured party. They understood that the two other climbers from the party of the victim were also staying overnight with him and that equipment would be needed for three members of the victim's party as well as themselves, so they packed six sleeping bags, six thermarest pads, two tents, stoves, food, fuel, extra clothes, and first aid equipment. Sean, Phil and Luke started up the Emmons Glacier a little after 1830.

As they climbed, it soon became apparent that Luke was traveling slower than Sean and Phil, and was indeed quite tired. After about two hours of climbing at the rate of 500 feet per hour (and reaching about 10,500 feet), Luke decided he was holding the other two back and that he shouldn't continue. At this point, Sean also learned via radio from Mike Gauthier at White River that the other two uninjured climbers in the victim's party had successfully descended the Disappointment Cleaver route to Camp Muir on the south side. Only the victim was left up high. The group redivided the equipment they were carrying, and Luke untied from Sean and Phil and descended with some of the excess equipment to Camp Schurman. At this point Sean and Phil were enthusiastic, eager to get on with the climb up to the injured climber at 13,400 feet.

Luke returned to Camp Schurman about 2130, planning to get some sleep. It was clear, cold, and blowing hard. Shortly after he returned, a group of five women arrived and started trying to set up a new North Face dome tent. Luke assisted them, and boiled water for them in the hut to try to get them warmed up. He returned to the hut, and was dozing off when Sean called White River at 2335. He reported that he and Phil had reached 12,900 feet and that one of them (very likely Phil) was having trouble with a crampon. They were about 500 vertical feet below the injured climber. At 2400 White River Ranger Station called for Sean with no response after three tries. They called again at 0030, and again received no answer. When White River called for Sean at 0100 with no response once again, Luke decided that they were in real trouble and that he needed to do something. Luke found another set of crampons and a smoke grenade in the Camp Schurman hut, joined a climbing party at 0200, and left for the accident scene a second time. This time he reached 11,500 feet before becoming ill. He handed the crampons and smoke grenade off to members of the climbing party, and again descended to Schurman, arriving there at 0500. White River again called Sean at 0530 with no response.

About 0700 Climbing Ranger Jennifer Erxleben and other rangers climbing from Camp Muir reached the injured climber at 13,400 feet, found that he was in good condition and out of the wind, with adequate clothing, food and fuel. They quickly realized that Sean and Phil had not arrived, and notified White River of this. They also arranged for a helicopter evacuation of the injured climber. An Army Chinook came in at 0900, picked up the injured Craver, and deposited two more Climbing Rangers near the summit who joined in the search for Sean and Phil. Craver was flown to Good Samaritan Hospital in Puyallup.

About 1000 the Chinook came back with Climbing Ranger Mike Gauthier on board and began assisting in the search. A short time later Sean and Phil were spotted from the air at the 12,000 foot level at the foot of a small cliff. Around the same time, Climbing Rangers found slide marks at 13,200 feet directly above the location of their bodies, and the climbing party to whom Luke had given the crampons and smoke flare found a part of a crampon and a blue ice ax (both of which turned out to belong to Phil Otis). The Chinook picked up the bodies of Ryan and Otis about 1100. (Source: *Bergtrage*, Seattle Mountain Rescue, Number 146, January 1996).

Analysis

Icy conditions, inexperience and faulty equipment all played a role in the deaths.

"Even the best climbers, had we sent them, could have met a tragic end under those conditions," said John Krambrink, chief ranger at Mount Rainier National Park. The two rangers confronted one problem after another, but were determined to prevent John Craver's death from exposure. They fell when they stopped at 13,200 feet to fix their equipment on August 12.

Otis had climbed Mount Rainier once and Mount Baker once, while Ryan had climbed Mount Rainier 11 times. They had enough experience to handle a rescue under less severe conditions, Krambrink said. But "I don't think any of us would have sent (Otis) up there had we known what the conditions were."

Otis did not thrust his ice ax deep into the snow and snap his rope to it, a technique most climbers use for an anchor, the report said. His ax was later found with only the tip in the snow. Also, one of the crampons didn't fit his boot properly, and the other had broken in half and was no longer screwed in tightly.

In their last radio contact, Ryan said Otis was having trouble with his crampons. He used duct tape and then white athletic tape to try to secure them, the report says.

Otis probably found the park-owned crampons in the hut at Camp Schurman, the base camp for ascents up the northeast face. (Source: From a report issued by an eight member panel of National Park Service employees and independent climbers who reviewed Mount Rainier National Park's internal investigation)

FALL ON ROCK, EXCEEDING ABILITIES
Washington, North Cascades, Liberty Bell
On August 14, Stim Bullit (75) and I (47) were climbing the third pitch (I led the first two pitches)—a crack above a ledge. Stim got to the crux of the 5.8 crack, couldn't figure it out and backed down. I volunteered to try to lead it, couldn't figure out how to climb the crux either, so I began to down climb. I fell while down climbing. My feet slipped off the wall. The protection held well, but my right leg apparently took full force of the fall on a ledge or other protrusion. After the injury, my leg would not hold my weight. We rappelled to the base of the climb; I bivouacked and Stim left and drove to phone mountain rescue people.

Analysis
I'm not a skilled technical climber and have never led above 5.7. I have done only a few top roped 5.8 pitches. My partner is much better technically and has led up to 5.9. In the hot flush of summit fever, I allowed desire to overcome judgment, exceeding my limit, and paid the price.

My repeated training in Mountaineering First Aid was very helpful. It allowed me to remain calm, set up a comfortable bivy, treat myself for shock, and even sleep until rescuers came. As much as I complain about getting recertified every three years, it's worth it. (Source: Kathy O'Toole)

FALL ON SNOW/ICE, MODERATE EXPERIENCE
Washington, Mount Rainier
On August 20, Scott Porter (32), Karl Ahrens (35) and Brian Nelson (32) were descending the upper Emmons Glacier after summiting. SMR members Kim Klasch and Bob Schumaker were on standby duty at Camp Schurman. At 1405 Klasch was watching parties on the route when he saw the group of three begin falling about the 13,400 foot level. They slid and fell about 2,400 feet down to the 11,000 foot level before coming to a stop in a crevasse. Klasch, Schumaker, and a Park Service Ranger left Camp Schurman

at 1440 to climb to the fallen climbers. In the meantime they had notified the Park Service of the accident. A Park Service rescue team was flown to the accident scene, and accomplished the rescue before Klasch, Schumaker, and the Park Service Ranger from Schurman could reach the scene. They directed another off-route party of two back onto the standard route and assisted them down to Schurman.

Porter and Ahrens were killed in the fall. Nelson survived. He was flown from the Emmons Glacier to Sunrise, and from there to Madigan Army Medical Center in Tacoma via an Army helicopter. From Madigan, Nelson was moved to Swedish Hospital in Seattle on August 24, where he was reported to be in critical but stable condition. It was his third climb on Mount Rainier. (Source: *Bergtrage*, Seattle Mountain Rescue, Number 146, January 1996)

(Editor's Note: Other than various people saying that the conditions were very icy, there were no other conclusions drawn in any of the NPS reports or newspaper articles received.

This accident brought the total number of fatalities on Mount Rainier to 67. Over the past 40 years, 258 people have died while mountain climbing in Washington State. Before the fall the previous week on Mount Rainier, the last fatal accident occurred in 1992. The worst climbing accident in U. S. climbing history in terms of total fatalities was in 1981 when ten climbers were buried by a large avalanche on the Disappointment Cleaver route.

There were a few other reports of accidents on Mount Rainier for the year, two involving falls on snow that could not be successfully stopped before an injury occurred, and one other involving crampons in which the victim cut his leg badly enough to require evacuation.)

FALL ON ROCK
West Virginia, Seneca Rocks, West Face
On August 20, Kel Young was leading "The Prune" at Seneca Rocks. He had placed protection above the small ledge which is just below the finish of the second pitch. After a couple of moves, he fell, toeing the ledge as he went by it. He was lowered to the ground with assistance from another party and evacuated by litter due to a fractured ankle.

Analysis
The second pitch of "The Prune" is notorious for doing in ankles here at Seneca. The count is two for the season so far. The small ledge just below the "Old Man's Traverse" ledge is a comfortable stance from which to place protection. Unfortunately, the vertical nature of the climbing above this stance almost ensures that in the event of a fall one will "toe" the ledge as one goes by it. (Source: John Markwell)

VARIOUS FALLS ON ROCK, MOSTLY CLIMBING UNROPED OR NOT ANCHORED
Wisconsin, Devil's Lake State Park and Peninsula State Park
Reports from Devil's Lake State Park provide an interesting contrast to the Shawangunks in that the average age of the climbers involved in the nine accidents reported for 1995 was 21. The youngest, which was a fatality, was an 11-year-old. He was at the top of a climb, alone, while his uncle was belaying his sister up. He was not tied in, and though

he had been warned earlier by other climbers about putting himself in a poor position, he apparently did not understand or accept the situation. At this age, close supervision is usually required. There was one accident in Peninsula State Park, which is not a climbing area, but was being used by an adventure training group for corporate team building. The victim, an experienced climber, was setting up a rappel and fell 70 feet. This accident was one of six that were the result of being unroped or not anchored when the fall occurred. There were four serious head injuries as a result of not wearing a climbing helmet in these cases. (Source: Jed Williamson and reports from Steven Schmelzer, Park Ranger, Devil's Lake State Park)

OVERDUE
Wyoming, Grand Teton National Park, Grand Teton
On July 5, Douglas Hall (26) left at 0600 to scout out the North Face route of the Grand Teton for a future ascent, and return via Garnet Canyon by the Dike Col/Teepee Glacier traverse. About noon, he decided to ascend the East Ridge route of the Grand Teton. He crossed into the top of the Molar Tooth's south gully about 1600. He thought about descending, but then decided to go for the summit. He traversed west on ramps into the next gully (Jackson/Johnson Route), and after encountering difficult climbing, he decided to rappel down the gully to Teepee Glacier. About 150 feet above the glacier, his rope became stuck, and he was forced to spend the night without bivy gear due to darkness.

On the morning of July 6, he down climbed some snow, then 100 feet of rock, and arrived at Teepee Glacier. He descended to the Jackson Hole Mountain Guides' high camp, where he was given snacks, and then continued his retreat to the valley floor. At 1012, he was met by Rangers Bill Alexander and Eric Gabriel about two miles from the Lupine Meadows parking area. The rangers had been dispatched as part of the rescue/search operation after Hall was reported missing by Kathy Pike at 0800 that morning. Hall was escorted by Alexander to the Jenny Lake Rescue Cache and interviewed. (Source: George Montopoli and Bob Irvine, SAR Rangers, Grand Teton National Park)

(Editor's Note: This was one of several "overdue" callouts which resulted in no injury or need for rescue beyond the search. For a different kind of outcome, see the September 18 report from Grand Teton National park.)

FALL ON SNOW, UNABLE TO SELF-ARREST, CLIMBING UNROPED
Wyoming, Grand Teton National Park, Teewinot
On August 1, Pamela Foyster (36) was descending the east face of Teewinot. About 1315 she fell while plunge-stepping down the snow which leads down from the big notch near the summit. She failed to self-arrest and tumbled out of control for approximately 50 feet to the bottom of the snowfield and then bounced another 50 feet down the rock.

Ms. Foyster was then assisted to the valley by two other climbers, Greg and Louise Smith. They arrived back at Lupine Meadows shortly before 2000. Foyster said that being a nurse, she had evaluated her own injuries and would seek medical attention the following morning. She had multiple bruises and possibly a fractured right arm. Her climbing helmet also suffered serious damage. (Source: Bob Irvine, SAR Ranger, Grand Teton National Park)

FALL ON SNOW, UNABLE TO SELF-ARREST
Wyoming, Grand Teton National Park, Grand Teton

Clay Roscoe (26) and Megan T. Piper (25) traveled down from Montana on July 30 and spent the night in the Bridger Teton National Forest at Station Creek, located in the Snake River Canyon. About noon on July 31 they came to the Jenny Lake ranger station where they obtained an overnight camping permit for Garnet Canyon. At that time the unusually snowy conditions on their proposed route—Owen-Spalding—were discussed, as was the advisability of having crampons and ice axes. They left the trailhead around 1500 and arrived at the Moraine camping area in Garnet Canyon four hours later. They were well equipped for this particular climb: overnight gear, including sleeping bags and bivouac sacks; synthetic pile clothing and water/wind-proof outerwear; climbing helmets; a significant climbing rack; ice axes; food; etc. Additionally, they had rented crampons.

Roscoe and Piper left their campsite around 0530-0600 on the morning of August 1 for their climb. Upon reaching the area above the Black Dike just west of the Needle, they decided to follow tracks up and west into the couloir known as the "Idaho Express," located west of the normal Owen-Spalding route. Utilizing this couloir, they reached the Upper Saddle about noon. The climb to the summit from this point took the pair two hours. While descending, they were roped up and wearing their crampons. Since they had only one rope with them, they joined another party for the 120 foot rappel to the Upper Saddle. After the rappel, Piper and Roscoe roped up again (short-rope technique, about 20 feet apart; Roscoe in the rear carrying the extra coils with a butterfly knot to his harness, Piper tied into her harness at the end of the rope with a figure-of-eight follow through knot). They descended to and then down past the Upper Saddle and then continued down to the rock island located on the eastern side of the "Idaho Express" couloir. Roscoe then set up a rappel on the eastern side of this rock island. But then they decided not to rappel, and therefore dismantled the anchor and coiled their rope. Roscoe placed the rope on the pack that he was carrying and they then discussed the best way in which to proceed from that point. Roscoe stated that Piper preferred descending the couloir to the east (the actual Owen-Spalding route), while he wanted to descend the route that they had utilized on the way up—the "Idaho Express." They eventually decided upon the latter.

Piper was wearing crampons and Roscoe was not. Piper was approximately 15 feet above Roscoe as they both stepped out to the west onto the steep snow in the couloir. Roscoe stated that as he looked up at Piper, "She didn't look good." He also stated later that her crampons may have been balled up with snow. At that point she slipped, fell, and made no attempt to self-arrest. Roscoe attempted to grab her as she went by and was pulled off his feet with her. It is difficult to say how far this initial slide on snow actually was as there were numerous footprints and slide marks in the area. Roscoe stated that he thought they had gone about 20-25 feet before hitting the initial rocks, but the on-site investigation pointed to this initial slide as being as much as 200 feet. At any rate, as they slid into the rocks at the bottom of the snow, Roscoe stopped and Piper continued down the couloir for another 300 feet. This area is located immediately west of and slightly above a short pinnacle which marks the point at which they had entered the couloir some hours earlier.

Roscoe traversed east through the notch located just above the pinnacle and proceeded down the snow slope at a high rate of speed at times losing control of his descent. At this time he did not have any climbing equipment with him. He jumped over the first overhang that he encountered (about 25 feet) and then down climbed to the east around the second. Roscoe stated that he "kept seeing scuff marks with a drop of blood." Lower in the couloir he completely lost control, got in a runnel, and slid all of the way to the bottom. He was screaming for help at this time and kept searching in hope of finding Piper.

At some point, during his descent of the couloir that he was in, Roscoe's cries for help were heard by an Exum Mountain Guides group who had just arrived at the Lower Saddle (1630). The guides in this group included Jim Nigro, Stephen Koch, Wes Bunch and Doug Chabot. Upon their arrival at the Guides' hut at the Lower Saddle, a cellular phone call was placed to the Exum office. I received a call from Exum office personnel at the Jenny Lake ranger station around 1640 which indicated that there was the possibility of an injured climber(s) somewhere above the Lower Saddle.

After receiving the cellular phone call from Exum guide Doug Chabot (which followed the initial call concerning cries for help) in which he stated that he "sees one person walking around way down in Dartmouth Basin and that he doesn't see anyone else," I requested the contract helicopter to be dispatched to the Lupine Meadows helibase. I also began assembling members of the Jenny Lake rescue team. After the helicopter landed at Lupine, an initial briefing was conducted. At 1800 rangers Springer and Alexander were flown to the south side of the Grand to conduct an initial aerial reconnaissance. Additional information from Exum guides at the Lower Saddle indicated that we were looking for a female who had fallen down the "Idaho Express." Roscoe and Exum guides Chabot and Bunch were quickly located in Dartmouth Basin and it was determined that he was ambulatory and able to climb back up to the Lower Saddle with assistance. The focus of the rescue effort was then directed toward the upper portions of the couloir where his partner had fallen. After searching this area for approximately 17 minutes, the helicopter landed at the Saddle with Springer and Alexander. Ranger Jim Woodmencey, on a patrol in Garnet Canyon, arrived at the Lower Saddle to assist with rescue efforts at this time. After the helicopter arrived at Lupine, doors were removed from the aircraft to improve the visibility for searching during the aerial recon. At 1839 the helicopter took off for the Saddle with rangers Perch and Benham aboard. At the same time rangers Springer and Alexander along with Exum guide Stephen Koch started climbing up from the Saddle on foot to conduct a ground search.

Throughout this portion of the rescue operation, plans were made for additional personnel to be flown up to the search area. A helicopter short-haul plan was discussed and appropriate equipment was assembled in case that option were to become necessary. At 1919 ranger Springer and Exum guide Koch located the victim in a moat at an elevation of 12,200 feet in the "Idaho Express" couloir. Springer moved the victim from her head-down position and attempted to find carotid and sub-sternal pulses for approximately 40-50 seconds, but he was not able to detect any pulse. Springer also attempted to listen for any sign of respirations and found none. He reported that the victim had trauma to the head and neck area with deformity and that there was obvious deformity to one leg. Because of the obvious rockfall hazard to rescue personnel, it was decided to terminate further recovery efforts until the morning when there was the best chance of having colder and safer conditions. The status of the victim and the decision to terminate the recovery effort at this point were discussed with Park Medical Advisor Lanny Johnson and he concurred with the decision. All rescue personnel returned to the Lower Saddle hut to spend the evening. At 2034 helicopter

46N returned with Roscoe to the Lupine Meadows helibase. He was interviewed and transported to St. John's Hospital in Jackson where he was admitted for treatment. His injuries included lacerations to his hands and wrist and numerous abrasions.

On August 2, beginning about 0700, rescue personnel returned to the recovery site. The victim was raised approximately 15 feet and then lowered about 300 feet to a suitable sling load site. At 1005 helicopter 46N left Lupine and a sling load operation was conducted and completed by 1030. Rescue personnel were returned to the Lupine helibase by 1400.

Analysis

Roscoe and Piper had both been climbing and mountaineering for five to seven years. They were both very fit individuals having rowed at a near Olympic level during their college years. Neither climber had received any formal instruction in snow and ice climbing techniques, yet both had made ascents in the Pacific Northwest—Piper of Mounts Baker, Adams and Hood (possibly a couple of times each) and Roscoe of Baker. Both had ascended Granite Peak, the highest in Montana. Roscoe had also climbed in the Beartooth and Crazy mountain ranges in Montana and in Chile near Portillo in 1994. The Grand Teton was their first experience in the Teton Range.

According to Roscoe, they were in a "very good state of mind" during this particular trip. There had been no recent disagreements between them, and they had been living together in Oregon for "five years and two months."

The fact that they were off-route during their ascent from the Lower Saddle to the Upper Saddle is noteworthy. Many people, however, make this same "mistake." The "Idaho Express" couloir appears to be (and is, in fact) a very direct route to the Upper Saddle. The pair had climbed a number of the snow and glacier-covered peaks in the Northwest, so a snow-filled couloir, although steep, may have looked enticing. They were being cautious on the way down, wearing helmets and staying roped up during the technical portion of the descent. At the bottom of the rappel they once again put the rope on, and used the short-rope technique with the strong person (Roscoe) in the back should a fall occur. There was a discussion as to which way to go at one point during their descent and ultimately they decided to go back down the way they had come up. The choice of the route with which they were familiar (even though it certainly is not the easiest descent route) deserves some merit. They made the decision to put the rope away just prior to the accident. This decision may, at least, have prevented a double fatality. Certainly most of the climbers who choose to descend from the Grand Teton in this same area are unroped as well. The snow that balled up in Piper's crampons definitely could have contributed to her fall. And finally, Roscoe's decision to reach out and help Piper, even though that precipitated his fall, simply shows how much he wanted to avert what became a great tragedy. It is worth noting that Piper did not attempt to perform a self-arrest and that they both lost their ice axes.

In conclusion, Piper and Roscoe possessed the technical skills to attempt the route, were well equipped and were in the process of descending the mountain in a cautious manner when this unfortunate tragedy occurred. A crampon balling up with snow, not engaging in an instantaneous execution of a self-arrest, and the attempt to try to grab and stop the falling partner are certainly factors that contributed to this accident. It may simply point out to all of us that the mountain environment has inherent risks, even if we are doing everything "right." (Source: Renny Jackson, SAR Ranger, Grand Teton National Park)

LOSS OF CONTROL—VOLUNTARY GLISSADE, FALL ON SNOW
Wyoming, Grand Teton National Park, Amphitheater Lake

Grand Teton National Park dispatch received a phone call at 1345 on August 4, from Josh Howell who was requesting assistance for an injured climbing partner near Amphitheater Lake. Dispatch transferred the call to ranger Perch who was the SAR coordinator for the day. Howell reported that Harold Brown (62) had injured his left arm and shoulder and lacerated his abdomen with an ice ax after falling approximately 300 feet on snow and impacting the rocks below. The incident had occurred at 1315. He was calling from a cellular phone that he had borrowed from hikers at Surprise Lake. Four other partners remained with the patient at the accident site. Howell agreed to return to the patient with the phone and wait for NPS assistance.

Bryan Dean, another member of the climbing party, continued down the trail and reported the incident in person at the Moose Visitor Center at 1431.

Medical control Lanny Johnson was notified of the incident and the reported injuries and concurred that a helicopter response was appropriate. Classic Helicopter pilot Mike Doster arrived in helicopter 46N and transported rangers George Montopoli and Andy Byerly to a heli-spot near Amphitheater Lake at 1427. Rangers Leo Larson and Bill Culbreath were transported on a subsequent flight. After reaching the patient Montopoli treated Brown for his injuries and hypothermia and lowered him approximately 300 feet down a scree slope to the heili-spot. Park rangers and other members of the climbing party were used for the lowering operation. Montopoli was transported with the patient by helicopter to St. John's Hospital in Jackson at 1637. The remaining rescue team members were transported by helicopter to Lupine Meadows and returned to the rescue cache by 1730.

Brown sustained a badly fractured scapula, two broken ribs and a pneumothorax. Additionally he received a minor laceration on his abdomen from the ice ax. He was admitted to St. John's Hospital for several days for treatment and observation. Brown was wearing a climbing helmet, which probably saved him from more serious injury.

Analysis

The party had intended to climb on Mount Owen that day but for various reasons they changed their plans and "played around" on the snow near the notch above Amphitheater Lake. The party was descending on snow and four members of the group had glissaded to the bottom. Brown was cutting steps in order to descend until another. member of his party convinced him to glissade as the others had done. He sat down to glissade and almost immediately realized that it was not a wise decision. He believes that using the ax to brake changed the direction of his slide. Brown attempted to perform an ice ax arrest one time but was unsuccessful. He began to tumble down the snow slope and in doing so cut his abdomen with the ice ax. The ax was lost even though it was attached to his wrist with a strap. After a slide of approximately 300 feet Brown hit some rocks sustaining various injuries. He hit his head but was wearing a helmet which prevented injury.

Brown said that he had been climbing for about 30 years and had climbed in the Teton range before. Previous climbs included the Owen-Spalding route on Grand Teton., He has climbed extensively on snow, but not recently. Brown has had to use his ax to stop a slide before and has always been successful. At the time of the incident he was wearing boots but not crampons.

Brown was a climber experienced in snow travel and chose to glissade against his better judgment due to encouragement from his climbing partners. Though experienced in the use of an ice ax, he was unable to successfully execute an ice ax arrest after gaining speed. (Source: Rick Perch, SAR Ranger, Grand Teton National Park)

FALL ON ROCK, CLIMBING ALONE AND UNROPED, NO HARD HAT
Wyoming, Grand Teton National Park, Teewinot
Keith Hensler (64) was supposed to pick up a friend, Lance Brown, at the Lupine Meadows trailhead on the afternoon of September 4. When Brown arrived at the trailhead about 1830, Hensler's car was there, but Hensler was not. Brown became concerned about his missing friend and notified dispatch around 2100. The rescue coordinator was notified and he decided to postpone further investigation until the following morning, since it was already dark and no one knew which direction Hensler had gone.

At 0715 on September 5, rangers Byerly and Culbreath were diverted from the Garnet Canyon trail to the east side of Teewinot while rehab crew members Wise, Bywater and Vergilio started up the Teewinot apex trail to search. Hensler's body was found by Byerly and Culbreath at 0950 at the 11,200 foot elevation on the east face route on Teewinot. He had apparently died as a result of a fall.

The body was retrieved in a sling load at 1210 using the contract helicopter, a 206L3 piloted by Mike Doster.

Analysis
Following a September 8 mountain patrol on Disappointment Peak and the Teton Glacier area, rangers Mark Magnuson and Robert Irvine traversed onto the East Face of Mount Teewinot to further investigate the scene of the Hensler fatality; specifically, to locate and retrieve the ice ax that was presumed to have been in the possession of Hensler at the time of his accident.

Upon locating the accident scene at approximately the 11,400 foot elevation (slightly higher than the original estimate), Magnuson and Irvine searched the area. At a point approximately 150 to 200 vertical feet above the ledge where Hensler's body was found, a light colored object was observed in a crack. This object was likely the same item observed at the time of the body recovery and reported to be a faded yellow sling. However, further investigation—aided by a monocular—determined this item to be the shaft of a wooden ice ax. The ax was at the top of a steep chimney, aligned with the likely "fall line" that the victim would have taken during his fall. Upon retrieval of the ice ax (which required 5.6 climbing moves), a billed ball cap was also located, approximately 20 to 30 feet below the ax. The head of the ax was positioned in a crack as if it had been intentionally placed or "hooked" there. Given the difficult terrain above the top of this chimney, it seems likely that Hensler was attempting to *ascend* this steep headwall. The location of the accident is, to confirm what was reported by rangers Byerly and Culbreath, a good 100 yards north of the East Face route. (Source: Mark Magnuson, SAR Coordinator, Grand Teton National Park)

(Editor's Note: In a follow-up interview with Lance Brown, it was learned that the climbing plans had changed due to Keith Hensler's having experienced severe stomach cramps—from drinking double strength Gatorade—on September 1 during their ascent to Surprise Lake. They returned to Lupine Meadows the next day, but Mr. Hensler felt bad about having to cancel his trip, so he offered to buy his friend a guided trip on the Grand with Exum Mountain Guides. While Mr. Brown did this climb on September 3 and 4,

Mr. Hensler made the decision to do the solo attempt.

There is a certain amount of psychological preparation needed for climbs. When plans change and a new objective is chosen—especially if it is in haste, achieving a good frame of mind may be sacrificed for the sake of following a schedule.)

OVERDUE
Wyoming, Grand Teton National Park, Grand Teton

On the afternoon of September 18, rescue coordinator Mark Magnuson was notified of three overdue climbers on the North Face of the Grand Teton. A check of the trailhead found the subjects' vehicle still in the parking lot. According to the reporting party, roommate and co-worker Lauren Gaylord, the group of three—George Stacy (26), Todd Walther (27), and Adrian Foreman (29) had left Jackson just before noon on Saturday, September 16. Their intent was to climb the North Face route and return home on the 17th via Garnet Canyon. As of noon on September 18, they had not returned home and had missed work.

Rangers located the party's vehicle still parked at the Lupine Meadows Trailhead. A check of permits for additional information revealed that the group had not signed out for the overnight, as required by park regulations. An investigation was initiated, including efforts to locate other climbers who had been on the North Face during that period of time. Through this process limited additional information was obtained. Ranger Leo Larson was sent to a vantage point on the Teton Park road with a spotting scope, but was unsuccessful in locating any persons or clues on those portions of the North Face route visible through the scope.

Contact was made via radio with ranger Sara Levson, who was hiking up Garnet Canyon for an overnight at the Platforms. She had not seen the party in question. Climbers descending from upper Garnet Canyon had not seen a group matching the description of the three.

With approaching inclement weather, the complexity of the North Face of the Grand Teton, and information obtained regarding the experience level and equipment of the climbers, Magnuson requested the Yellowstone contract helicopter at 1600 to respond to Lupine Meadows to initiate a reconnaissance flight of the intended route. At 1700, just prior to the Yellowstone helicopter's arrival, the overdue climbers contacted park dispatch by telephone from Dornan's. (Rangers had left a note on their vehicle instructing them to call as soon as possible if they returned.)

Analysis

A follow up interview of the three climbers by rangers Magnuson and Jackson found the following information: Stacy, Walther, and Foreman departed Jackson at 1100 on September 16 to climb the North Face of the Grand Teton. They hoped to climb the first four pitches of the route and bivouac on the first ledge that night. Due to a late start, long approach, slow climbing progress, and route-finding problems, they were forced to spend the first night at the top of the third pitch on a marginal ledge. They continued climbing on the 17th but encountered similar problems, spending that night on the lower section of the second ledge. It then took them until 1300 on the 18th to traverse off the second ledge to the upper saddle. They stated that they expected to find rangers at the Lower Saddle patrol hut to report their status, but none were there. (Rangers Gary Wise and Bill Culbreath had just departed that morning.) They continued hiking down Garnet Canyon, arriving at the trailhead around 1700. Regarding their failure to obtain a permit, they said they weren't aware that permits were still required to climb.

Magnuson issued Stacy, Walther, and Foreman each an optional appearance violation notice for failure to obtain a permit for an overnight back country stay/bivouac. This regulation is posted at two different locations at each trailhead, in the park brochure and newspaper, and at permits offices. Additionally, seasonal press releases and special notices clarifying that permits are still required for all overnight trips, including those by climbers, were noted as posted in the Jenny Lake Ranger Station and several locations throughout the community. (Source: Mark Magnuson, SAR Coordinator, Grand Teton National Park)

FALL ON ROCK, CLIMBING UNROPED, PARTY SEPARATED, EXCEEDING ABILITIES, NO HARD HAT
Wyoming, Grand Teton National Park, Cascade Canyon

On September 23, at 2230 Grand Teton dispatch received a call from Mike Shaw (23) reporting his partner, Keith Berlin (24) was missing after the pair had become separated while rock scrambling in Cascade Canyon. Berlin had scrambled up a rock outcropping ahead of Shaw but was not there when Shaw arrived at the same location. Shaw decided that the climbing above there looked too difficult for him and returned to the base of the outcropping. When Berlin did not return, Shaw explored the area, calling Berlin's name for two or three hours but did not receive a response.

At 0030 on September 26, Shaw returned with Rangers Gabriel and Wise to Berlin's last seen location, an area of fractured rock buttresses separated by steep talus near the base of Storm Point's southeast side approximately three quarters of a mile west of Inspiration Point. Gabriel and Wise searched the area for three hours by headlamp but were unable to locate Berlin.

At 0820 an eight member NPS team with two search dogs began searching the area between the Symmetry Couloir drainage and the south face of Storm Point. At 1100 the Bridger-Teton contract helicopter (46N) was called to assist with the search by performing aerial reconnaissance with three spotters on board.

At 1125 Ranger Morris found Berlin among some boulders located several hundred feet up the hill north of the trail. Berlin had evidently fallen a significant distance off a nearby rock outcropping not long after he was last seen by Shaw. Berlin complained of head, neck and hip pain, had sustained facial lacerations and displayed a diminished level of response. Berlin was immobilized with a cervical collar and full body vacuum splint and placed in a litter. After two non-technical lowerings, he was taken down the trail to the west shore boat dock. Berlin was shuttled across Jenny Lake by boat and then transported by ambulance to St. John's Hospital in Jackson. He was treated for injuries that included a crushed lumbar vertebrae and a significant concussion. (Source: Renny Jackson, SAR Ranger, Grand Teton National Park)

OFF ROUTE, STRANDED, CLIMBING ALONE, INADEQUATE EQUIPMENT/CLOTHING, EXCEEDING ABILITIES
Wyoming, Grand Teton National Park, Middle Teton

On the morning of September 29, Jenny Lake Subdistrict Ranger Mark Magnuson received a report of an overdue climber on the Middle Teton. According to the reporting party, Susie Struble, Aaron Gams (25) departed his Wilson residence mid-day on September 27 intending to climb the Glacier route and return home late on the 28th. He did not return home as planned and missed work that night.

At noon on September 29, a hasty search team located overnight equipment belonging to Gams, stashed at the Meadows. Search efforts were escalated that day, involving 18 field personnel and the establishment of a base camp at the Meadows. Search progress was hampered by a severe early season winter storm, eliminating helicopter support as an option. An incident overhead team was established and planning for the next operational period accomplished.

On the morning of September 30, an additional 41 personnel had joined the search effort, with field deployment following an 0700 briefing. At 1300 a team of Jenny Lake climbing rangers summitted the Middle Teton via the Southwest Couloir and made voice and visual contact with Gams. Gams was stuck on a small ledge on the northwest side of the mountain, approximately 100 feet below the summit. Ranger Bill Alexander was lowered to Gams and the two were raised to the summit by a mechanical advantage system. Efforts to rewarm Gams included hot drinks and heat packs. He was then lowered down the southwest couloir on belay, then by litter, to a helicopter landing zone on the bench north of the South-Middle Teton saddle. This arrival coincided with the first available window of flyable weather, and Gams was flown from the mountain by the park contract helicopter. He was transported to St. John's Hospital by vehicle where he was admitted for hypothermia, frostbite, and exhaustion.

According to Gams, he climbed the Glacier Route as planned on the 28th, but became off-route below the summit. He wandered across the north face and ridge to the northwest couloir. Below the summit of the peak he became ledged out, unable to continue up or retreat. Gams survived two days and two nights on a small ledge, in severe winter conditions, with minimal gear.

Analysis
On October 2, ranger Mark Magnuson interviewed Aaron Gams in his room at St. John's Hospital. Gams was new to the Jackson area, arriving two to three weeks before the accident. He had been sharing a house in Wilson, WY.

On the morning of September 27, Gams left his residence in Wilson with plans to climb the South and Middle Teton. Arriving at the Moose Visitor Center around noon, he purchased a guide book authored by Richard Rossiter, "Teton Classics." Following a quick review of routes he approached the permits office desk stating that he wished to climb the Glacier Route on the Middle Teton. At that time, ranger Jean Lawrence issued Gams an overnight use permit for the south fork of Garnet Canyon. Gams then departed Lupine Meadows Trailhead, arriving at the Meadows by late afternoon or early evening. Gams chose to camp in the Meadows rather than continuing up to the south fork of Garnet.

Gams left his camp about 0530 on the 28th, arriving at the base of the Glacier Route around 0700 to 0830. He climbed the route to the Dike Pinnacle col, then turned west toward the summit. He then climbed a steep, narrow snow couloir, north of the summit pinnacles, that took him across the north face to the northwest couloir. Gams realized he was off-route. He then looked up the northwest couloir and, thinking it appeared reasonable, started up. Below the summit the route steepened and turned to hard ice, at which time he elected to exit left into a chimney, climbing on rock. Gams said he did not have the proper equipment to climb the last section of the northwest couloir. He had single leather boots with hinged crampons and one ice ax. Gams continued up this chimney on low fifth class rock which he described as "hard and exposed." Just short of the summit—60 to 100 feet—he encountered a steep headwall (estimated at 5.7) that was beyond his skill level. After exploring options, Gams determined that he was now unable to continue up or retreat back down the chimney. By mid-afternoon, he resigned himself to being rescued. Gams said he knew that a weather system was approaching but did not know the extent of the forecasted storm.

Gams said he spent the next two nights on a small ledge measuring approximately four feet by ten inches wide. He was clothed in two light-to-medium-weight layers of synthetic clothing with a shell jacket and pants, wearing a stocking cap and gloves. An additional medium-weight jacket was found in his pack, which he had not worn. (Gams stated that he didn't realize this jacket was in his pack.) He had minimal food and water. (Source: Mark Magnuson, SAR Coordinator, Grand Teton National Park)

(Editor's Note: Close to 60 people needed for this one impresses me, and brings to mind Yosemite's use of citing some climbers under 36 CFR 2.34 (a) (4): Creating a Hazardous Condition.

As we were going to press, we received two reports of incidents from Devil's Tower National Monument, one of which resulted in a fatality from a fall while trying to retrieve a stuck rappel rope; the other was a case of heat stroke. This party was not carrying adequate water, and they were also cited for failing to register for their climb.)

TABLE I
REPORTED MOUNTAINEERING ACCIDENTS

	Number of Accidents Reported		Total Persons Involved		Injured		Fatalities	
	USA	CAN	USA	CAN	USA	CAN	USA	CAN
1951	15		22		11		3	
1952	31		35		17		13	
1953	24		27		12		12	
1954	31		41		31		8	
1955	34		39		28		6	
1956	46		72		54		13	
1957	45		53		28		18	
1958	32		39		23		11	
1959	42	2	56	2	31	0	19	2
1960	47	4	64	12	37	8	19	4
1961	49	9	61	14	45	10	14	4
1962	71	1	90	1	64	0	19	1
1963	68	11	79	12	47	10	19	2
1964	53	11	65	16	44	10	14	3
1965	72	0	90	0	59	0	21	0
1966	67	7	80	9	52	6	16	3
1967	74	10	110	14	63	7	33	5
1968	70	13	87	19	43	12	27	5
1969	94	11	125	17	66	9	29	2
1970	129	11	174	11	88	5	15	5
1971	110	17	138	29	76	11	31	7
1972	141	29	184	42	98	17	49	13
1973	108	6	131	6	85	4	36	2
1974	96	7	177	50	75	1	26	5
1975	78	7	158	22	66	8	19	2
1976	137	16	303	31	210	9	53	6
1977	121	30	277	49	106	21	32	11
1978	118	17	221	19	85	6	42	10
1979	100	36	137	54	83	17	40	19
1980	191	29	295	85	124	26	33	8
1981	97	43	223	119	80	39	39	6
1982	140	48	305	126	120	43	24	14
1983	187	29	442	76	169	26	37	7
1984	182	26	459	63	174	15	26	6
1985	195	27	403	62	190	22	17	3
1986	203	31	406	80	182	25	37	14
1987	192	25	377	79	140	23	32	9
1988	156	18	288	44	155	18	24	4
1989	141	18	272	36	124	11	17	9
1990	136	25	245	50	125	24	24	4
1991	169	20	302	66	147	11	18	6
1992	175	17	351	45	144	11	43	6
1993	132	27	274	50	121	17	21	14
1994	158	25	335	58	131	25	27	5
1995	168	24	353	50	134	18	37	7
Totals	4515	677	8127	1492	3854	535	1096	235

TABLE II

Geographical Districts	1951–1994			1995		
	Number of Accidents	Deaths	Total Persons Involved	Number of Accidents	Deaths	Total Persons Involved
Canada						
Alberta	322	98	698	16	5	32
British Columbia	249	97	542	2	0	4
Yukon Territory	32	26	69	1	0	4
Ontario	28	6	52	3	2	6
Quebec	25	5	54	0	0	0
East Arctic	7	2	20	0	0	0
West Arctic	1	1	2	0	0	0
Practice Cliffs[1]	13	2	18	0	0	0
United States						
Alaska	340	134	486	15	9	39
Arizona, Nevada Texas	56	8	104	1	1	2
Atlantic–North	616	95	1032	40	1	75
Atlantic–South	60	15	92	3	0	8
California	886	220	1877	28	6	34
Central	95	9	156	11	1	18
Colorado/Oklahoma	552	171	938	17	3	32
Montana, Idaho South Dakota	57	22	89	3	0	4
Oregon	118	57	292	10	3	21
Utah, New Mexico	102	33	180	7	1	15
Washington	873	258	1550	19	8	41
Wyoming	421	96	761	13	3	34
Artificial Walls	2	0	2	0	0	0

[1]This category includes bouldering, as well as artificial climbing walls, buildings, and so forth. These are also added to the count of each state and province, but not to the total count, though that error has been made in previous years.

(*Editor's Note: The Practice Cliffs category has been removed from the U.S. data and replaced with Artificial Walls.*)

TABLE III

	1951–94 USA	1959–94 CAN.	1995 USA	1995 CAN.
Terrain				
Rock	3252	384	117	14
Snow	1957	293	43	4
Ice	172	78	8	6
River	12	3	0	0
Unknown	22	6	0	0
Ascent or Descent				
Ascent	2957	410	113	12
Descent	1789	274	54	12
Unknown[3]	246	3	1	0
Immediate Cause				
Fall or slip on rock	2147	205	77	7
Slip on snow or ice	725	148	29	4
Falling rock, ice or object	451	104	16	1
Exceeding abilities	357	27	24	0
Avalanche	247	103	2	2
Exposure	225	12	6	0
Illness[1]	246	20	9	0
Stranded	221	46	18	2
Rappel Failure/Error	173	29	15	4
Loss of control/glissade	159	15	5	0
Fall into crevasse/moat	122	37	3	1
Failure to follow route	109	18	4	2
Piton pulled out	83	12	1	0
Nut/chock pulled out	82	3	6	0
Faulty use of crampons	55	5	3	0
Lightning	39	6	0	0
Skiing	41	9	3	0
Ascending too fast	43	0	0	0
Equipment failure	5	2	0	0
Other[2]	151	15	22	3
Unknown[3]	58	8	1	0
Contributory Causes				
Climbing unroped	858	139	17	4
Exceeding abilities	813	153	6	1
Inadequate equipment/clothing	513	66	18	2
Placed no/inadequate protection	387	51	30	0
Weather	354	42	8	4
Climbing alone	298	52	9	1
No hard hat	205	21	11	1
Nut/chock pulled out	154	16	6	0
Darkness	105	14	5	1
Party separated	92	16	3	0
Piton pulled out	82	10	0	0

	1951–94 USA	1959–94 CAN.	1995 USA	1995 CAN.
Contributory Causes (cont.)				
Poor position	96	12	7	1
Inadequate belay	92	12	8	6
Failure to test holds	63	16	2	2
Exposure	53	10	1	0
Failed to follow directions	53	5	3	0
Illness[1]	29	4	3	0
Equipment failure	8	4	1	0
Other[2]	207	79	13	4
Age of Individuals				
Under 15	110	11	2	0
15-20	1112	193	11	3
21-25	1347	221	45	1
26-30	955	185	40	1
31-35	562	92	26	1
36-50	746	104	54	3
Over 50	116	16	8	2
Unknown	811	429	25	37
Experience Level				
None/Little	1429	269	20	13
Moderate (1 to 3 years)	1280	334	23	6
Experienced	1216	350	70	13
Unknown	1294	241	81	18
Month of Year				
January	170	10	3	2
February	168	36	7	1
March	228	41	8	1
April	307	27	13	1
May	672	42	11	1
June	786	50	18	1
July	866	206	29	3
August	774	117	37	2
September	1015	46	20	10
October	306	29	17	1
November	146	5	3	0
December	58	16	2	0
Unknown	4	0	0	0
Type of Injury/Illness (Data since 1984)				
Fracture	664	111	69	9
Laceration	296	43	36	3
Abrasion	172	35	10	2
Bruise	177	49	31	1
Sprain/strain	160	13	10	5
Concussion	86	11	23	1
Frostbite	70	4	6	2
Hypothermia	73	10	10	0

Type of Injury/Illness (cont.)	1951–94 USA	1959–94 CAN.	1995 USA	1995 CAN.
Dislocation	57	6	7	0
Puncture	25	3	0	1
Acute Mountain Sickness	13	0	1	0
HAPE	46	0	1	0
CE	11	0	3	0
Other[1]	154	26	19	1
None	58	3	24	28

[1]These include: a) exhaustion (6); b) atrial fibrillation; c) gastrointestinal bleeding; d) myoscopic hematoma (2); e) hypothermia (7); f) possible umbilical hernia; g) frostbite (2); h) dehydration (6); i) severed spinal cord; j) torn meniscus; k) neurological damage–head; l) 50 bee stings; m) flail chest; n) lacerated pancreas; o) ETOH; p) heatstroke.

[2]These include: a late start (5); b) wet rock (3); c) haste to: complete route (5), to meet a schedule, to catch thieves raiding packs at bottom, and to get to the bar; d) crowded route–rock fall; e) cornice collapse (2); f) trying to catch ice ax dropped from above; g) lost balance–tripped (3); h) over confident; i) bees (2); j) rope jammed while prussiking–stranded; k) unable to self-arrest; l) fell while setting up rappel (2); m) misperception–route research; n) failed to follow directions (2); o) inadequate supervision; p) poor navigation (2); q) fell attempting to retrieve stuck rappel ropes.

[3]Probably a fall–on Mount Hood.

(Editor's Note: Under the "other" category, many of the particular items will have been recorded under a general category. For example, the climber who fell into his unanchored partner knocking him off would be coded as Fall on Rock, Falling Rock/Object, and Placed Inadequate Protection.. The point in this category is to provide the reader with some added detail. It should be apparent that many of these details can be translated into a few basic categories.)

MOUNTAIN RESCUE ASSOCIATION OFFICERS

Tim Cochrane, *President*
PO Box 115
Vail, CO 81658

Tim Kovacs, *President*
PO Box 4004
Phoenix, AZ 85030

John Wehbring, *Secretary/Treasurer*
4980 Pacific Drive
San Diego, CA 92109

Don Adamski, *Member at large*
6734 W. Multnomah Blvd.
Portland, OR 97223

Rod Willard, *Member at large*
PO Box 3732
Estes Park, CO 80517

MOUNTAIN RESCUE ASSOCIATION, INC.
200 Union Boulevard, Suite 430-1355
Denver, CO 80220

MOUNTAIN RESCUE GROUPS IN NORTH AMERICA

(Where not obvious, area covered is indicated in parentheses)
°Indicates membership in Mountain Rescue Association

ALASKA

Alaska Mountain Rescue Group,° PO Box 241102, Anchorage, AK 99524
U. S. Army Northern Warfare Training Center,° Fort Greeley, AK, APO Seattle 98733
Denali National Park Ranger Station, Talkeetna, AK 99676

ALBERTA

Banff Park Warden Service, Banff National Park, PO Box 900, Banff, Alberta T0L 0C0
Jasper Park Warden Service, Jasper National Park, PO Box 10, Jasper, Alberta T0E 1E0
Kananaskis Park Warden Service, Kananaskis Provincial Park, General Delivery,
    Seebe, Alberta T0L 1X0 (Alberta outside National Parks)
Waterton Park Warden Service, Waterton National Park, Waterton, Alberta T0K 2M0

ARIZONA

Arizona Mountaineering Club Rescue Team, PO Box 1695, Phoenix, AZ 85030
Central Arizona Mountain Rescue Association,° PO Box 4004, Phoenix, AZ 85030
Grand Canyon National Park Rescue Team,° PO Box 129, Grand Canyon, AZ 86023
Southern Arizona Rescue Association, Inc.,° PO Box 12892, Tucson, AZ 85732
Sedona Fire Dept./Technical Rescue Group, PO Box 3964, West Sedona, AZ 86340

BRITISH COLUMBIA

Columbia Mountain Rescue Group, Royal Canadian Mounted Police, Invermere,
    B.C. V0A 1K0 (East Kootenays)
Glacier Revelstoke Park Warden Service, Glacier Revelstoke National Park, PO Box
    350, Revelstoke, B.C. V0E 2S0)
Kootenay Park Warden Service, Kootenay National Park, PO Box 220, Radium Hot
    Springs, B.C. V0A 1M0
Mountain Rescue Group, c/o Frank Baumann, PO Box 1846, Squamish, B.C. V0N
    3G0 (Coast Range, Northern Cascades)
North Shore Rescue Team,° 165 East 13th Street, North Vancouver, B.C. V7L 2L3
YoHo National Park Warden Service, Box 99, Field, B.C., Canada V0A 1 GO

CALIFORNIA

Altadena Mountain Rescue Team, Inc.,° 780 E. Altadena Drive, Altadena, CA 91001
    (Los Angeles County)
Bay Area Mountain Rescue Unit, Inc.,° PO Box 6384, Stanford, CA 94309 (Northern
    Sierra Nevada)
China Lake Mountain Rescue Group,° PO Box 2037, Ridgecrest, CA 93555 (Southern
    Sierra Nevada)
De Anza Rescue Unit, PO Box 1599, El Centro, CA 92243 (Imperial Valley, Baja)
Inyo County Sheriff's Posse,° PO Box 982, Bishop, CA 93514
Joshua Tree National Monument SAR,° 74485 National Monument Dr., Twenty-nine
    Palms, CA 92277
June Lake Mountain Rescue Team,° P. O. Box 436, June Lake, CA 93529
Los Padres Search and Rescue Team,° PO Box 30400, Santa Barbara, CA 93130

Malibu Mountain Rescue Team,° PO Box 222, Malibu, CA 90265
Montrose Search and Rescue Team,° PO Box 404, Montrose, CA 91021
(Los Angeles County)
Riverside Mountain Rescue Unit,° PO Box 5444, Riverside, CA 92517
(Riverside County)
Saddleback Search & Rescue Team, PO Box 5222, Orange, CA 92667
San Diego Mountain Rescue Team,° PO Box 81602, San Diego, CA 92138
San Dimas Mountain Rescue Team,° PO Box 35, San Dimas, CA 91733
San Gorgonio Search & Rescue Team, San Bernardino Sheriff, San Bernardino,
CA 92400 (San Bernardino Mountains)
Santa Clarita Valley Search and Rescue,° 23740 Magic Mountain Parkway, Valencia,
CA 91355
Sequoia-Kings Canyon National Park Rescue Team,° Three Rivers, CA 93271
Sierra Madre Search and Rescue Team,° PO Box 24, Sierra Madre, CA 91025
(Southwestern United States, Baja, California)
Yosemite National Park Rescue Team, Inc.° PO Box 577, Yosemite National Park,
CA 95389

COLORADO
Alpine Rescue Team, Inc.° PO Box 934, Evergreen, CO 80439 (Front Range)
Colorado Ground Search and Rescue,° 2391 S. Ash Street, Denver, CO 80222
Crested Butte Search and Rescue,° PO Box 485, Crested Butte, CO 81224
El Paso County Search & Rescue, Inc.,° PO Box 9922, Manitou Springs, CO 80932
Eldorado Canyon State Park,° PO Box B, Eldorado Springs, CO 80025
Garfield Search & Rescue,° PO Box 1116, Glenwood Springs, CO 81602
Grand County Search & Rescue,° PO Box 172, Winter Park, CO 80482
Larimer County Search & Rescue,° PO Box 1271, Fort Collins, CO 80522
Mountain Rescue—Aspen, Inc.° PO Box 4446, Aspen, CO 81612 (Western Slope)
Ouray Mountain Rescue Team, PO Box 220, Ouray, CO 81427 (Gunnison National
Park, Rio Grande National Forest, Uncompahgre Park)
Rocky Mountain National Park Rescue Team,° Estes Park, CO 80517
Rocky Mountain Rescue Group, Inc.,° PO Box Y, Boulder, CO 80306
San Juan Mountain SAR, PO Box 4, Silverton, CO 81433
Summit County Rescue Group,° PO Box 1794, Breckenridge, CO 80424
Vail Mountain Rescue Group,° PO Box 115, Vail, CO 81658
Western State Mountain Rescue Team,° Western State College, Gunnison, CO 81231

IDAHO
Idaho Mountain Search and Rescue,° PO Box 8714, Boise, ID 83707
Palouse-Clearwater Search and Rescue,° Route 1, Box 103-B, Troy, ID 83871

MAINE
Baxter State Park Mountain Rescue Team,° 64 Balsam Drive, Millinocket, ME 04462

MONTANA
Glacier National Park, SAR Coordinator, West Glacier, MT 59936
Lewis and Clark Search and Rescue,° PO Box 473, Helena, MT 59601

NEW HAMPSHIRE
Appalachian Mountain Club, Pinkham Notch Camp, Gorham, NH 03581 (White
   Mountains)
Mountain Rescue Service,* PO Box 494, North Conway, NH 03860

NEW MEXICO
Albuquerque Mountain Rescue Council,* PO Box 53396, Albuquerque, NM 87153
St. John's College Search and Rescue Team, 1160 Camino de Cruz Blanca, Santa Fe,
   NM 87501 (Northern New Mexico, Southern Colorado)

NORTHWEST TERRITORIES
Auyuittuq Park Warden Service, Auyuittuq National Park, Pangnirtung, N.W.T.
   X0A 0R0

OREGON
Alpinees, Inc.,* 3571 Belmont Dr., Hood River, OR 97301 (Hood River County)
Corvallis Mountain Rescue Unit,* PO Box 116, Corvallis, OR 97339 (Central
   Cascades)
Crater Lake National Park Rescue Team, PO Box 7, Crater Lake, OR 97604
Ellesmere Island Warden Service Ellesmere Island National Park and Reserve P.O. Box
353, Pangnirtung, NT, XOA ORO
Eugene Mountain Rescue,* PO Box 10081, Eugene, OR 97401 (Oregon Cascades)
Hood River Crag Rates,* 1450 Nunamaker, Salem, OR 97031
Portland Mountain Rescue,* PO Box 1222, Portland, OR 97207

UTAH
American Search Dogs,* 4939 Benlomand, Ogden, UT 84003
Rocky Mountain Rescue Dogs,* 9624 S. 1210 E., Sandy, UT 84070
Salt Lake County Sheriff Search and Rescue,* 2942 Cardiff Road, Salt Lake
   City, UT 84121
Zion National Park*, Chief Ranger, Springdale, UT 84767

VERMONT
Mountain Cold Weather Rescue Team, Norwich University, Northfield, VT 05663
Stowe Rescue Squad, Stowe, VT 05672

VIRGINIA
Appalachian Search and Rescue Conference*, PO Box 430, Flint Hill, VA 22627
   (Blue Ridge and Shenandoah Mountains and Southwest Virginia)

WASHINGTON
Bellingham Mountain Rescue Council*, PO Box 292, Bellingham, WA 98225
   (Whatcom County)
Central Washington Mountain Rescue Council*, PO Box 2663, Yakima, WA 98907
   (Washington)
Everett Mountain Rescue Unit*, PO Box 2566, Everett, WA 98203 (North Central
   Cascades)

Mount Rainier National Park Rescue Team°, Longmire, WA 98397 (Mount Rainier National Park)

Seattle Mountain Rescue°, PO Box 67, Seattle, WA 98111 (Washington)

North Cascades National Park Rescue Team°, 2105 Highway 20, Sedro Woolley, WA 98284

Olympic Mountain Rescue°, PO Box 4244, Bremerton, WA 98312 (Olympic Range, Cascades)

Olympic National Park Rescue Team°, 600 Park Ave., Port Angeles, WA 98362 (Olympic National Park)

Skagit Mountain Rescue Unit°, 128 4th St., Mount Vernon, WA 98273 (Northern Cascades)

Tacoma Mountain Rescue Unit°, 7910 "A" St., Tacoma, WA 98408 (Central Washington, Cascades, Olympics)

WEST VIRGINIA

Gendarme/Seneca Rocks Climbing School, PO Box 23, Seneca Rocks, WV 26884

WYOMING

Grand Teton National Park Mountain Search and Rescue Team°, PO Box 67, Moose, WY 83012 (Grand Teton National Park)

Mountain Rescue Outing Club, University of Wyoming, Laramie, WY 82071 (Wyoming)

YUKON

Kluane Park Warden Service, Kluane National Park, Haines Junction, Yukon Y0B 1L0